In Search of Lost Knowledge

William Grove

Visit us online at www.authorsonline.co.uk

A Bright Pen Book

Copyright © William Grove 2011

Cover design by William Grove & Jamie Day ©

All rights reserved. No part of this publication may be reproduced, stored in a retrieval system, or transmitted in any form or by any means, electronic, mechanical, photocopy, recording or otherwise, without prior written permission of the copyright owner. Nor can it be circulated in any form of binding or cover other than that in which it is published and without similar condition including this condition being imposed on a subsequent purchaser.

British Library Cataloguing Publication Data.
A catalogue record for this book is available from the British Library

ISBN 978-0-7552-1305-4

Authors OnLine Ltd
19 The Cinques
Gamlingay, Sandy
Bedfordshire SG19 3NU
England

This book is also available in e-book format, details of which are available at www.authorsonline.co.uk

I S O L K

In Search of Lost Knowledge.
Old Mysteries - New Concepts.

The following pages contain subjects, which my inquiring mind selected for thorough investigation, subjects, some of which have been covered by others without satisfactory conclusion.

The Sumerian King-lists

Stonehenge with its seemingly insignificant circles of holes.

The question of how such enormous pieces of stone were erected.

The Round Table in accordance with the account by Layamon.

Valhalla with its five-hundred and forty gates.

The Vishnu Epic.

A similar huge span of time from the records of Chaldean priest/historian Berossus.

Fresh light upon the construction of Solomon's Temple.

Arthur of legend.

The Lady Godiva.

Other subjects that continue to intrigue.

W. G. Grove

Antecedents.

Throughout Greece of Old many triads are to be discovered that relate to the Triple Goddess in one form or another. We find the moon divided into three aspects, those of the two crescents, both waxing and waning, and our satellite at the glorious full. There were three seasons; three individual goddess-names each one representative of the same lunar deities as Maiden, Nubile Nymph and Wise Old Crone, also of Birth, Life and Death. She, the Great Mother, varied in name in accordance with tribe and vicinity in which she was worshipped. There is, too, the ritual of the Thrice-ploughed Field and the fire drill with its triple-armed swastika disk to act as a weight which improved the drill's efficiency.

In Welsh legend, at a time when male gods were gaining ascendancy over female counterparts, a divine hero appears whose name is Gwengwyngwyn, which means Thrice White One, an epithet better attributed to the lunar goddess since white is her generic colour. Artemis is Of the Three Ways and, as Maiden, takes the colour white.

Irish tradition informs us that, during the latter half of the third millennium BC, there were invasions by people who seem to have come from lands bordering- the Aegean Sea. Some arrived overland whilst others took to sea-routes. Among these invaders were the Round Barrow makers.

Tribal movement, in the Near East, forced people to flee with the intention of settling elsewhere in peace. Due to such upheavals, in their homeland, Pelasgians, from the vicinity of the Black Sea, reached Ireland around 1500 BC. These people followed a matriarchal system of rule, presided over by the Goddess Danae. They came via Denmark, which country continues to bear memory of Danae in its name and that of its people, the Danes. Using Briton, then called Albion, as a stepping stone, they landed in Ireland where they became known as the

Danaans. It is from that name that we get the masculinized Don, and Donnus of a later date. Local Irish called them the Tuatha de Danaan.

A further invasion took place by tribes from Thrace, which persuaded some among the earlier arrivals, to move on to northern Albion by the Tuatha de Danaan. These last invaders settled in Scotland, probable ancestors of the Picts. At approximately 1250 BC more people arrived on Irish shores. They were the Miletians who claimed descent from Apollo. Apollo, twin brother to Artemis/ Britomartis, originated in the Aegean City of Miletus, the Cretan one being favoured. The route, taken by them, is said to be westward through the Mediterranean Sea to a spot near to Greek Gades, today's Spanish Cadiz.

When one recalls so much early movement of people from Britain to Ireland, and the reverse, it is no surprise to find cultural links in their respective traditions.

Welsh god Bran, the name meaning Crow, Raven, and Alder, too, a tree associated with Death, a tree to be found guarding sepulchral isles of the past - had a sister Branwen - White Crow as against Black Crow. The White Crow was sacred to Greek Athene, it's colour being lunar.

Greek Aesculapius was burnt to death by a jealous Zeus. However, when a child Aesculapius had been rescued from a fire in which his Earthly parents had perished., Bran, too, was destroyed by a jealous foe, one Evnissyen. In Welsh legend Bran's nephew is burnt to death, too. Achilles is wounded in the heel by a poisoned dart. Bran is hit in the heel by a poisoned dart. Aesculapius bedded fifty girls in a single night. Bran does likewise with the Isle of Man women. But he tops the Greek heroes' record by one hundred. Bran, of course, is ancestor to that other man of legend, King Arthur, in himself non-too selective in his choice of numerous bed-companions of the female gender.

There is an Amathaon, whom Robert Graves equates with a sea-goddess., Amathaounts, stole the Dog and Roebuck from out of the Underworld, we are informed through Irish folklore.

During his Twelve Labours, Greek Heracles stole the Dog, Cerebus, and the White Roebuck of Artemis, from out of the Underworld. Anyone who upset Artemis, Actaeon for instance, was due to be sacrificed at the winter solstice. The Dog, incidentally, symbolises various lands of the Middle East.

Why should people, from the Aegean vicinity, not have reached the British Isles? Others had been doing so since the Early Stone-age.

Archaeological evidence traces these last from as far away as Lidya, people less culturally-advanced than the later Pelasgians. Long ago there was a general westward and northward tribal movement throughout Europe in general.

Europe- *Europa, loved by Zeus*- given by Greeks the meaning of Far-ranging. Other countries, through which early people advanced, are Spain and Portugal from as far as the Baltic, and to our own islands too. The oldest of megalithic structures bear witness to this, to be seen along Western European coastlines, including Brittany.

Much has been learnt, concerning the earliest of people from burial procedures, funerary furniture and stone-axe styles. And what of those blue faience beads manufactured in Egypt some 1380 to 1350BC? Some of those beads have been unearthed in Wiltshire, imported during that era.

There have been attempts to link latter stages in the construction of Stonehenge trilithons with the Mycenaean culture. It is a fact that faience beads have been discovered in lands to which the Mycenaeans came. They were great travellers, were they.

Robert Graves describes the Irish burial tomb at New Grange as being one of that country's Fortresses of the Sidhe, which latter are to be associated with Irish magicians.

New Grange is a round barrow built entirely of stone covered with pebbles of white quartz, as practised by Bronze-age people in honour of the Goddess. With sunlight reflected off the tomb's surface it would appear to be like brilliant glass, or a very bright moon, it being circular.

Throughout Britain such burial-caves had entrances opened up on the Eve of Samhaine, or All-Saints Eve of later date. This is strictly in keeping with Greek practices at their Feast of the Dead.

Graves goes on to say that this type of beehive construction reached Ireland via Spain and Portugal, some four or more thousand years ago. Spiral patterns, carved into the stones of New Grange, have parallels in Mycenaean Greece. One-depiction shows a ship with high prow and stern, plus a single, large sail. This design of boat is typical of Minoan Crete.

That the New Grange entrance is aligned with sun-rise at midsummer's day, is in keeping with dolmens sited across southern France from the Rhone to the Languedoc-. They are there in their hundreds, all aligned with major sun-positions on the horizons, varying from equinoxes to solstices.

The white quartz covering at New Grange would have given rise to Glass Castles of legend. Those who see Glastonbury Tor as being such a Glass Castle, largely by the first element in the name, should recall that William of Malmesbury wrote that the name is rooted in a Saxon Glasteing, the name of a family that lived in the area.

Saxon Glas can mean any colour from pale-green to azure blue. If Irish and Welsh Glass Castles are seen to be surrounded by water reflecting bright daylight, or the deep-blue of the night, perhaps they do have a point, although Glastonbury Tor is bald of white quartz, nor is it the burial tomb of Arthur and Guinevere. Surely such greatly-esteemed personalities deserve a far more resplendent place of entombment?

Glastonbury has been linked with Arthur's Avalon even though there is no trace of former forests of apple-trees in the area, and, what is more, all Orchards of the Hereafter had entrances guarded by a Wise Serpent, of which last there is no trace in local folklore.

****

Robin Hood had his twelve archers, and Robin Hood took part in a Greenwood marriage with his woodland nymph, Maid Marion. That takes us back into a very-distant past through numerous Maries, Marians, Mariamnes, and Maris, the last three being goddesses.

Heracles, too, had his twelve archers, you may note. Heracles took part in his own Greenwood marriage to a woodland nymph. He was also sacrificed at the end of his allotted six-months, one year, eight-years or nineteen-years in accordance with how early or late he lived as consort to the Goddess.

Heracles moved around clad in a lion-skin, carrying a club of oak. One is reminded of that gigantic, Dorset chalk-figure whose first creators obviously realized that gods are not in need of lion-skin clothing.

Just as Heracles rescued Theseus from the Underworld did Arthur's page, Gorue, rescue his master. Gorue was also Arthur's cousin as are all Greek Heroes in one fashion or another. In many cases they are the same Hero.

According to one Welsh bard his namesake Taleisin accompanied Arthur into the Underworld, and was one of the Seven who returned. Be they Irish, Welsh or Greek those Underworld forays were tests such as those engaged in the Mysteries would undergo.

Graves takes the name Taleisin and equates it with a variety of Greek roots, Tla, Atl, Atlas and Atlantis, all containing the same three letters of the alphabet. Primitive equivalents of Heracles/Hercules exist. He is known as Atlas Telamon. Then there are Talus, Telmon also spelt Tlamon.

When Bran was summoned, by the Goddess, to enter The Land of Youth, his talisman was an apple-branch. All Greek heroes, when about to be sacrificed to the Goddess, were given an apple as their passport to the Elysian Fields. Arthur went to the Apple Isle of Avalon to be cured of his wounds, they say.

There is a female character in Arthurian legend, by the name of Alice, wife of Alisander, who appears at Arthur's court. There is a goddess called Alys from which the name Alice is derived. Alys is, naturally, of Greek disposition

****

I here quote from Graves who quotes from one Diodorus Siculus who, in turn, repeats a statement from sixth-century BC Hecateus, Greek historian.

Diodorus Siculus: - *Hecateus, and some others who treat of ancient tradition, give the following account: Opposite the coast of Celtic Gaul is all island in the ocean, not smaller than Sicily, lying to the north, inhabited by Hyerboreans who are so-named because they dwell beyond the North Wind. This island is of a happy temperature; rich in soil and fruitful in everything, yielding its produce twice in one year. Tradition has it that Latona was born there and, for that reason, the inhabitants worship Apollo more than any other god. They are, in a manner, his priests for they daily celebrate him with continual songs of praise and pay him abundant honours. In this island is a magnificent Grove to Apollo, and a remarkable temple of round form adorned with many consecrated gifts. There is also a city, sacred to the same god, most of the inhabitant, of which are Harper's who continually play their harps in the temple and sing hymns to the god, extolling his actions.*

Hyperboreans use a peculiar dialect and have a remarkable attachment to Greeks, especially to Athenians and the Delians, deducing their friendship from remote periods. It is related that some Greeks

formerly visited the Hyperboreans with whom they left consecrated gifts of great value and, also, that in ancient times Abaris, coming from the Hyperboreans into Greece, renewed family intercourse with the Delians.

It is also said that, in this island, the moon appears very near to Earth, that certain eminencies of terrestrial fore are plainly seen in it, that Apollo visits the island once in the course of nineteen years, in which period the stars complete their revolutions. And for that reason the Greeks distinguish the cycle of nineteen years by the name of the Great Year. During the season of his appearance the god plays upon the harp and dances every night from the vernal equinox until the rising of the Pleiades. The supreme authority, in this city, and in the sacred precinct, is vested in those called Boreadae being descendants of Boreas, and their governments have been uninterruptedly transmitted in this line.

****

How complex becomes the whole structure or ancient history as it reaches us in the form of legend and true myth!

Hecateus was a truly observant chronicler. Where he refers to the nineteen-year Apollo cycle this is close correlation of lunar time against solar time, a period of 235 lunations and exactly nineteen years of the sun, precise to within 0.0061 of a lunation. This was the maximum duration in the life or a sacred king, a happy marriage between matriarchal and patriarchal societies, the moon being female, the sun male.

Hecateus seems to have been well informed; in Cornwall are two prehistoric circles of 19 stones. But, the round temple to Apollo could better indicate Stonehenge with its enticing *19 stones* of the Inner Horseshoe, which, in turn, present a stylised representation of a crescent moon.

Greek Latona is the Mother of Apollo. As such she would be mother to Artemis, twin, and once spiritual senior to Apollo. Artemis brings us the lunar goddess to whom sacrifice is made each 19 years at the midsummer solstice.

In Arthurian legend Apollo succeeds Lucius.

Could low-lying Salisbury be the city referred to by Hecateus? Place-names with the SAL element invariably point to a spot where willows grew alongside a river.

In the Beth Luis calendar of tradition the fifth letter is called Saille, or Sal. The fifth month is that of the willow, alphabetically a very important tree. It was from the willow that the five-fold bond was made, a device with which to truss the sacrificial victim, five being a number sacred to the Goddess. It is to be seen at the core of an apple cat transversely, that same fruit which was the sacred king's assured ticket to the Apple Orchards of Eternal Youth, the five-pointed star, that Temple to Apollo right upon their doorstep.

The Hyperhoreans worshipped Apollo, knew of the nineteen-year cycle, this being fixed as a length of reign after which the sacred king is sacrificed. Stonehenge is a temple, round and where lunar cycles both large and small, can he measured if only one knows the procedure involved.

Beyond the North Wind means literally that in terms of Greek knowledge of their world, which was quite extensive within the bounds of Europe and the Middle East.

****

When Arthur's knights were squabbling over precedence do they represent aspects of a lunar calendar that has become useless for no-one knows how to keep it true to lunar-time, the secret of which lies in numerical values to be detected in Stonehenge circles of holes and stones?

If anyone should doubt the Greek connection they should study Robert Graves' The White Goddess.

Now to the Greenwood.

We cannot escape the past. It lies there in traditional folklore, perhaps in elements of old poetry, the poetry of ordinary people, that of rural dwellers who pre-date such romantics as Grey who rested in total comfort whilst his Ploughman character sweat, mud-caked boots heavy, a tiring burden for legs working from dawn to dusk, up-field and down keeping the furrows straight as a sunbeam, personal pride in an ability artistic to the eye, his accomplishment, his lowly cottage-roof in need of a new thatch, his evening-meal bread and broth, leg of rabbit were he so fortunate. So much for Romantics.

So Humpty Dumpty was a huge, brass cannon, they say, one that fell from a castle-wall and shattered where it landed, far too fragmented for any king, with numerous men, to put back together again. That particular poem is like true myth in that it conceals an historic event.

Bards of Old were poets, those who memorized earlier, sacred history and passed it on, by word of mouth, to *apprentice-initiates* until others came along to employ the written word for a similar purpose, words so obscured that no-one, outside their brotherhood, would understand the message so contained.

But later folklore is equally cryptic, albeit the stuff of legend. And who better than Layamon to thus describe the Round Table of legend?

First to the name Mary, which, as of the Virgin, was originally spelt Marian in English, Pagan Marian, Sea-goddess of antiquity. There are variations of this name: Mariamne, Miriam, Myrrhine, Myrten, Myrrha, and Maria the patroness of poets and lovers, also mother of the Love-archer. Robert Graves tells us that Marian is the Mermaid, Mermaid overwritten as Merry-maid. She is the Love-goddess who rises from the sea, Aphrodite to the Greeks.

Crusaders discovered, in the Holy Land, unorthodox Christian sects, heretics to the established Church, they who taught of a Mari-Gypsy. Cults of the Mari-Gypsy reached English shores along with pilgrims who travelled to Compastella, in Spain, carrying with them, copies of apocryphal gospels, Mari-Gypsy/Aphrodite scallop-shells fixed to their hats, the badge of an unorthodox religions society.

During the Middle Ages Mari-Gypsy worship became so firmly established that it gave it's name to Merry (Mari) England.

Throughout England Mari-Gypsy thus became identified with the Saxon Love-goddess, the May-bride by virtue of the latter's association with the May-tree cults in which one may envisage the figure of Goddess Goda whom I discovered to have provided Godiva with her name. Later! She, Mari-Gypsy, is to be found in company with Merddin, Old Merlin his very self. Merddin became Robin Hood, when Christianized, and Robin Goodfellow, too.

Graves draws attention to the French Robin, generally regarded as a diminutive of Robert. In this context Robin means Ram or Devil. To this day, in France, a water-tap, such as one to which a hose pipe might be fit, is known as a Robinet because spouts of old fountains were shaped in the form of a ram's head, with horns. Robin Goodfellow is recalled as being a bit of a devil in his habit of performing merry tricks and foolish gestures.

Some British witches spoke of Robin when referring to their god. But why Robin, son of Art? Arthur, didst they take thy name in vain? Robin Hood, of Sherwood fame, is accepted as a real person, born at Wakefield during the late 13th century. He was in service to Edward111 from 1323 to 1324, and had a close relationship with May-day revels. His forester-father, Adam Hood, had his son christened Robert.

It was as Robin Hood that our hero renamed is wife Matilda, as Maid Marian, defiance, of ecclesiastic laws that turned Robin into a hero, among ordinary folk. The famous oak, in Sherwood Forest, may well have been a sacred tree from which the need-fire log would be cut at Yule, itself sacred to the pagan faith. *Hood* had the meaning of *Log*.

Greenwood marriages were known as Mad Merry, a popular version of Maid Marian.

Heracles, *Roman Hercules,* of course, long before the legendary Robin Hood did so, led his own band of twelve archers into the Greenwood where he married his own Maiden, although this is likely to be a coupling with a priestess-representative, in fact, of the Triple-goddess.

Since Morris, as in Morris Dancers, was formerly spelt Mari, and since they perform the Stag-dance of Old, one must ask forgiveness in suggesting that the dancers are merely revealing an aspect of the Mari-Gypsy cult practices.

The stag, in company with other animals, the hare, the roebuck, boar and bear, crow, wren of the bird family, and a variety of trees, among other forms of life, were important elements in ancient folklore. Each had it's meaning, esoteric, and frequently linked with a particular, even unusual, habit to be observed in a creature or portent of things to come in trees and other forms of natural growth. A first sighting of a kingfisher heralded fine weather to come. Swans, flying to north, might presage death in some form, these birds being under protection of the Goddess, she who decided upon the fates of men.

In a ballad, from the Robin Hood era, a pagan influence cannot be overlooked. It goes:

> *How many monthes are in the yeare?*
> *There are thirteen I say:*
> *The midsummer Moon is merriest of all,*
> *Next to the merry monthe of May.*

Thirteen is to be linked with the female, Beth Luis Nion tree-calendar, which is lunar as opposed to the later Boibel Loth tree-calendar and solar, one tree removed. May was a time when ritual-observance of the

Goddess was made, not necessarily upon May-day but to the nearest full-moon. Midsummer, too, was similarly important, especially for the carrying out of ritual sacrifice to whichever goddess was pre-eminent in the locality. This, too, would have been discharged at the full-moon nearest to the day of midsummer, this last to be judged from whatever local arrangement they employed to pin-point the passage of solar-time, in fact their natural calendar, or pre-historic alignment of stones whereby to foresee the approach of that day. Surprising is it not that the Vatican employs a lunar-related formula in calculations for the date of Easter-day?

In a later ballad the thirteen-months become twelve. There is no mention of midsummer nor moon. Thus we have further evidence of Robert Graves' *iconography*, the intentional revision of text, often for religious purposes, here the male promoted above the female, Eve being relegated to a lower status than Adam, just as Artemis was down-graded by Greeks with a preference for her male twin, Apollo, the Church again endeavouring to eraze any lingering attachment to goddess-worship in favour of it's own male deity. There is nothing new in the brain-washing of today.

For the Beth Luis Nion Tree Calendar, mentioned above, see An Extension of the Hyperborean Legend.

The Sumerian King-lists.

Historians maintain that the Sumerians gave us the first-known civilization. Those people had a superb knowledge of mathematics, the movement of stars and other remarkable attributes. Much has been learnt about them from clay tablets unearthed by the archaeologist trowel, examples of their knowledge recorded upon clay soft enough to take impressions from a wedge-shaped stylus to create that which is dubbed cuneiform writing. Hardened beneath a hot sun those tablets were preserved for thousands of years, from around 2,500 BC. It is from their tablets, known as the Weld-Blundell Prism that the king-lists came.

The Sumerians occupied an area to north of the Persian Gulf, abundantly irrigated by the Rivers Euphrates and Tigris.

The Sumerian King-lists is in two parts, the first of which covers the reigns of ten individual kings. The following 23 kings' combined lengths of reign are somewhat less outstanding compared with the first ten, respectively 24,510 against 456,000 solar years.

It was Erik von Daniken who equated those kings with beings from outer-space, with surprising knowledge of longevity. I would claim that our Erik should have looked much nearer to Planet Earth for the explanation.

I followed an instinctive hunch, when endeavouring to analyze such colossal figures. I divided 456,000 by 24,510, the answer being 18.604651. But, despite the hunch, that figure meant nothing to me, at the time.

Some time later I was studying a book upon astro-astronomy, wherein I came across that 18.604651 as being the number of years duration for one major lunar cycle, otherwise called a Major Lunar Standstill.

So the king-lists had provided a clue to what those awesome lengths of reign implied. In the same book was mention of Professor Gerald Hawkins work upon possible astronomical alignments at Stonehenge. The professor suggested, amongst other remarks, that the 56 Aubrey Holes, at Stonehenge, may well have been employed for measurement of lunar eclipses. I took mental note of that.

Elsewhere there was mention of the Major Lunar Standstills in relation to the 18.604651 figure.

I shall deal with only the first ten of those inimitable reigns for the simple reason that I have mislaid details of the remaining 23. Nevertheless, their apparent grand-total of years had enabled me to find a numerical key by means of which to gain clarification of the first ten. In fact, the 23 individual reigns, apart from their final aggregate, are otherwise pointless.

The first-ten kings' reigns in order of the original ………

Table 1.

Reign Number	Years
1	28800
2	36000
3	64800
4	43200
5	21000
6	18600
7	241200
8	36000
9	108000
10	28000

I made use of the words, *apparent grand total,* above with regard to the figure 456,000, this with good reason for a check upon the ten-reigns' actual quantity, reveals a figure of 625,600-years, a difference of 169,600 years. I was somewhat bewildered by this, wondering why the 456,000 number had been included? Patience added to further calculations, provided a likely answer. The larger quantity, even though tempting, did not assist in a decypherment of the precise nature of what was concealed within those quite extraordinary lengths of reigns, hence the 456,000?

I am unable to be certain but this riddle may be due either to an error upon the part of an archaeological translation or, more likely, a deliberate case of obfuscation by Sumerian scribes, as one finds to be in frequent use, where ancient legend and folklore are concerned.

These figures, remarkable though they appear in print, conceal a secret, mysticism from the past about to be raped of any magical content. To some degree they remind me of the fantastic quantities quoted in Plato's Atlantis dialogue. However, my pocket-calculator possesses a little magic of it's own. $456,000 \div 24,510 = 18.604651$. This divisor, I realized, would provide answers of high-numerical value, too high to make sense. I would have need of others if I were to unravel the secret in those ten reigns, assuming that there was one. Even so, I was increasingly confident that there was some arcane element there awaiting discovery.

There are those who would have us believe in an Egyptian year of 360-days, a misconception based upon it's 360 repetition in old texts. I shall not argue the point but, what does appear to have been the trend is that priesthoods made convenient use of a nominal 360-day year by which to make easier the regulation of intervals between religious events, which same 360 is a most convenient way for creation of sub-divisions in a circle, which is also a cycle. Surely they had a means whereby the remaining five-days could be absorbed, without upset to their 360-based calculations. There is the legend of Egyptian Isis gambling way 5-days from a 365-day year.

With a pope, wishing to force the Christmas festival into greater prominence over the Yuletide 12-days of pagan conviviality, deliberately losing 11-days from the extant Julian calendar, why should not an Egyptian priesthood lose 5-days, making them temporal against a remainder all encompassed with a religious framework? 5-days of no spiritual value to anyone, therefore to be ignored in any count of that nature?

And so to some fairly basic mathematics. Please note that figures, in columns 3 and 4, are a result of using quantities from column 2 twice over.

For example:
$$28,800 \div 18.604651 = 1548.$$
$$28,800 \div 360 = 80.$$

Table 2.

Column 1 Reign No	Column 2 Length of reign	Column 3 Divisor 18.604651	Column 4 Divisor 360
1	28,800	1548	80
2	36,000	1935	100
3	64,800	3483	180
4	43,200	2322	120
5	21,000	1128.75	670
6	18,600	999.75	51.666
7	241,200	12964.5	670
8	36,000	1935	100
9	108,000	5805	300
10	28,000	1505	77.777

Reigns 5,6 and 7, in Column 3, give answers to one and two-places of decimal whilst, in Column 4, reigns 6 and 10, have figures with recurring places of decimal. I had hoped it would be otherwise for simplicity of calculation. Nevertheless, there existed more than sufficient indications that I might be following a rewarding path.

If I were to solve all of the king-lists secrets, I had to know why some answers, above, were not of a whole-number variety?. Was there yet another relevant divisor?

I took a second look at each individual reign. They were all clearly divisible by 100, but not by 1,000. I then recalled that, in association with the moon, the planet Venus was also favoured by the Ancients, this at a time when existed lunar- goddess triads to be worshipped.

Planet Venus has a cycle of eight-years, as they were aware.

Venus is the sole one among our planets that forms a precise geometric design in it's five apogee-points during each of it's eight-year cycles, that is the five most-distant points it is seen to reach from Earth. Those five-points are those of a perfect pentagram, a sorcerer's pentacle.

Rightly or wrongly I decided to employ that figure 8 for my calculations, specifically when multiplied by 100, to give me 800. I was, after all, dealing with huge quantities.

Table 3.

Reign Number	Divisor 800 Result
1	36
2	45
3	81
4	54
5	26.5
6	23.25
7	301.5
8	45
9	135
10	35

Again, reigns 5,6 and 7 were not whole-numbers, although reign 10 now was. And 800 is precisely-divisible by 18.604651, answer 43.

Some, but not all answers, with the 800 divisor, were divisible by 9.

Why not divide oddity with oddity?

Table 2: I took 1128.75 from Column 3, and divided it by 58.333 Column 4, answer 19.35, whilst in Column 2 we have a 1935, ten-times greater. However, this type of calculation was not suited to other oddities in Table 2. Yet another route was required.

Although reign number 10 was now divisible by a whole-number. To be kept in mind is that 800 ÷ 18.604651= 43.

I added together reigns 5,6 and 7, Table 2, Column 2, on the off-chance that this approach might bring enlightenment.

21,000 +18,600 + 241,200 = 280,800.

I then introduced the first key-figure, 18.604651.

280,800 ÷ 18.604651 = 15,093.

This latter figure needed further reduction if it was to prove useful to the general design.

An analysis of 15,093 reveals that it consists of 117 x 129. I again reduced these divisors.
117 = 13x9
129 = 43x3.
That figure 43 will show itself to be of great value.

Had I realized, earlier, that 3 x 117 = 351, I would have used this last as a divisor. 15,093 ÷ 351 = 43, too.

Table 3:, the number 26.5, reign 5, when divided into 1128.75, ,reign 5, Column 3, Table 2, provides that 43 again.

To Table 2, once more, reign 10, 28,000 years with an answer of 77.7777, Column 4 is another oddity until given closer study.

28,000 ÷ 18.604651 and then by 77.7777 = 19.35, whereas in reign 2, quantity 36,000, when divided by 18.604651 the result is 1935, or 19.35 x 100.

1935 ÷ 43 = 45. In fact, in this mathematical manner, all ten reigns can be reduced to respective two-digit amounts, which may have significance since they may be possible lengths of fixed lengths in actual reigns.

By employment of divisors 18.604651 and 800, which last is 43 x 18.604651, in one pattern or another, round-figure answers can be found.

So I divided the 456,000 by 800 to equal 570. I did likewise with the 24,510- reign-total and the 570-figure, answer which surprised me with another 43.

The quantity 129 arose earlier; 24,510 ÷ 129 = 190, 3x190 = 570.

However, more to the point, as it was to transpire in connection with Stonehenge, 570 = 30 x 19, the 30 and 19, providing numerical connections, as does the 43.

Only by systematic observation of stars, sun, moon, other planets and the duration of their cycles, be they Sumerian, Ancient Brits, Cambodian following Indian influence, Norse man or woman, and others, could those Ancients pass on, to their successors, information, patiently-refined measures of time, seeing good or evil portents in the activities of astrological bodies forming magical designs in the night-skies.

They, too, would have seen the Plough, Ursa Major and Minor, Orion and company to which, no doubt, they applied whatever name they favoured. Therefore, separated by thousands of miles, among different nations people would reach some identical answers from a shared celestial clock.

Any among those Sumerian King-lists reigns, that is immediately divisible by 800, can be reduced to two-digit answers.

For example 36,000 ÷ 800 = 45 , itself open to further division, thereby the creation of fundamental spans of time, whether or not they relate to any king.

64800 ÷ 800 = 81, again open to further reduction.

Where a figure does not comply as a round-number following division, then, since the Sumerians had no decimal system, it required a treatment that would provide round-figure answers, as I reveal by addition of two or more oddities together.

Proof that these reigns refer to Lunar Standstill-cycles is further established, firstly through the mathematical implications to be found in those enigmatic holes at Stonehenge.

The Stonehenge Connection.

Across the British Isles, also in the Carnac vicinity of Brittany, France, much study of megalithic structures has brought convincing evidence that many of their pieces of stone, placed in position by pre-historic people, were erected to serve specific purposes, that of basic astronomy with particular observance of both solar and lunar cycles. There are many instances of such stones that were arranged in circles, some with out-rider stones for purpose of alignment with positions of the sun upon an horizon. Professor Thom travelled from stone circle to stone circle not seeking solar alignments but those of the moon. He discovered many instances that confirmed a pre-historic fascination with lunar sightings of this nature. He suggested that this was the case at Stonehenge.

Please bear in mind that the designers of the Stonehenge complex had no knowledge of figures to places of decimal-point. But I do in order to describe my theory.

My Sumerian King-lists calculations contain a number of divisors, one key-and several significant sub-divisors. I enumerate them as follow -

$$18.604551,$$
$$43.$$
$$30.$$
$$19.$$
$$800.$$
$$8.$$

Here the value 8 can be discarded. But retain the $30 \times 19 = 570$ from the king-lists calculations. In like fashion $800 = 18.604651 \times 43$.

Scholars are agreed that upright timber posts were set in position, at Stonehenge, for the purpose of establishing the most northerly point, upon the horizon, reached by the moon when rising to general NE at the site, a time when our ancient satellite would appear huge, and to hover there. This occurred every 18.604651 solar years, and is dubbed The Lunar Standstill.

I do not know how huge the moon would appear to the Sumerians at the Standstill, but they clearly knew of its hovering effect by virtue of that 18.604651(x43) period of solar years.

There exist circles of holes and stones at Stonehenge. The numerical values of these I, too, enumerate as follow -

43 in each of the Q and R circles of holes.
30 Y Holes. 30 vertical stones of the Sarsen Circle.
29 Z Holes. 56 Aubrey Holes.
59 stones of the outer Circle plus
19 stones of the Inner Horseshoe.

Among these figures are direct counterparts of the king-lists numerical divisors, 43, 30, and 19 .Of these 43 is the final figure to which I reduced individual reign of the first ten. Not only is 43 the number of holes in each of the Q and R circles, therefore twice, it is also to be seen in the Aubrey Holes 56, plus the 30 Y Holes which equal 86 or 43 x 2. I will remind you that the king-lists reveal 24510 ÷ 18.604651 = 570 which, in turn equal 30 x 19.

Further to that, 456,000 ÷ 570 = 800 which is 18.604651x43.

An illustration of the pair of concentric circles of 43 holes/stones-each at Stonehenge.

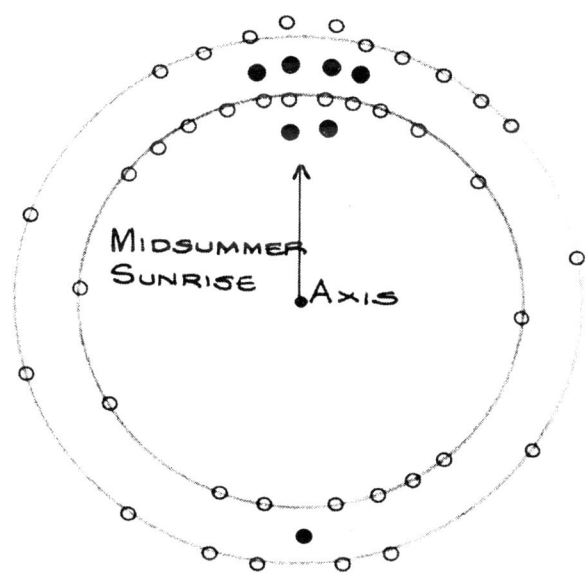

As is to be seen I do not represent all stones making up the 2 x 43 circles.

This arrangement, about 75 feet (22.5 M) in its larger diameter, was placed centrally to the remaining complex.

So far there is the suggestion that the Stonehenge astronomers held much in common with their Sumerian counterparts. So why the 56 Aubrey holes and also the 59 stones of the Outer Circle and the 29 Z Holes?

This 59 figure has now been precisely established, for it has been also considered to be 60, or 61. But 30 Y Holes plus 29 Z Holes equal 59.

If one accepts the direct correspondences, so far achieved, as not being mere coincidences, then it becomes plausible to consider that, for example, the 29 Z Holes were placed there to serve some solid purpose. To the 56 Aubrey Holes: 18.604651 is the number of years contained from one Lunar Standstill to the next. 56 ÷ 18.604651 = 3.01.

3.01 cycles of 18.604651 present an error of 0.01 of such a cycle. This is to be seen as 0.01 x 18.604651 which equals 0.18604651, which converts to 67.954672 days during a period of 56 solar years, an error that will grow with the passage of time, unless correction is available. The annual discrepancy would amount to 1.2134763 days. This latter number, when multiplied by 9 becomes 10.921287, almost exactly 11.0 days in 9 years, close to half of the Standstill cycle. So slight an error would be simple to adjust, at an appropriate date, to a fine degree of accuracy.

Here I wish to state that all calculations depend upon a sidereal year of 365. 25636-days., Y and Z Holes, numbering respectively 30 and 29 in numerical values: one lunar month consists of 29.5306 days. This figure, when doubled, equals 59.0612 days (a discrepancy of only 0.612, or 0.0306-days per lunation compared with the 59 Y and Z -holes quantity. 0.0306 days is equivalent of 44.064 minutes or, 1.5 minutes per day. This amounts to 9.0836 hours per solar year.
29 x 9.0836 = 263.4244 hours.

263.4244 ÷ 24(hours) = 10.976017 days in 29 years. I consider that an adjustment of 11.0 days at the end of each 29-year period would not have been outside the scope of Stonehenge astronomers.

Thus far I have, through process of mathematics shown some remarkable correlation's between the Sumerian King-lists figures and those to be deduced from the Stonehenge patterns of holes and stones.

No matter what the spoken tongue mathematics is a universal language, its basic formulae fixed and unchanging. The movements of planets and stars follow the same paths today as they did long before the appearance of the Sumerian culture, and in the same time-scales. Only the colour of Sumerian skins, and those of Stonehenge Britons, differs.

Within these pages I have dealt with the end result, and not the wonderful work expended in the movement of great pieces of stone by intelligent people who, in accordance with prevailing thought, not so many years in the past, were no better than the wild beasts the skins of which they wore.

I claim originality in this work, the result of which confirms that once our lunar orb was held in greater esteem than that of the Sun. Lunar-worship preceded that of the solar. In other words moon-goddesses were worshipped long before the arrival of sun gods on the scene.

The lunar cycle of 18.604651 solar years is fixed by the moon. It remains the same for all people, no matter where the observation-point from Asia to the British Isles.

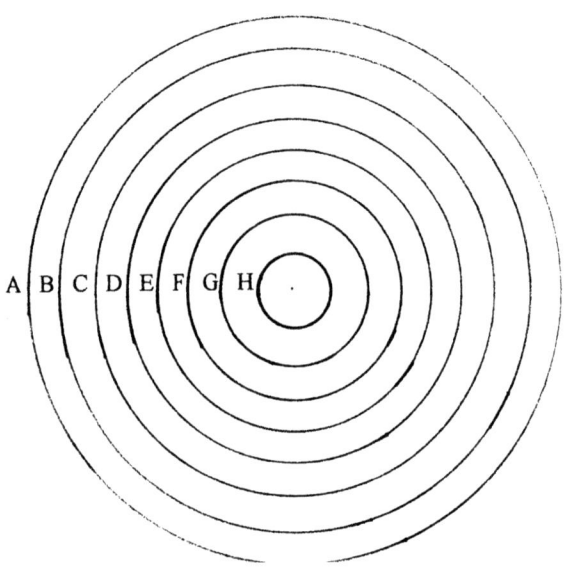

A wholly schematic representation of Stonehenge Circles and Horseshoes intended as a mathematical guide, only.

A denotes 59 holes for the Outer circle.
B denotes 56 Aubrey holes.
C denotes 29 Z holes.
D denotes 30 Y holes.
E denotes 30 holes for the Sarsen Circle.
F denotes 43 holes each for the Q and R holes concentric circles.
G denotes Outer Horse-shoe Trilithons.
H denotes 19 stones of the Inner Horse-shoe.

The same mathematical principles must apply for measurement of time, strict numerical correspondences existing between king-lists and Stonehenge being neither coincidence nor series of coincidences.

One solar-year consists of 12.368746 lunations.
12.368746 x 19 = 235.00617 lunations with 19 years a king-list divisor, a cycle of years discovered by Greek mathematician, Meton. 19 is also associated with Hyperborian Apollo's appearance-cycles at his northern temple.

Mathematics may be employed to prove all manner of theories not necessarily of the importance that may be attributed to them in whatever calculations might indicate. For example:

360 ÷ 29 = 12.423793. This resultant figure, given in degrees of arc might be thus employed:
12.423793 x 4 = 49.65172°s.
My source gives 50°s as being the solstice azimuths for Stonehenge. If that be today's figure then it would be a little less 4000 years ago. I do not, however, believe that the people of Stonehenge made use of their 29 holes for such a mathematical purpose

Yet More upon the Enigma that is Stonehenge.

Stonehenge, a monument of vast proportions, the earliest stage of which is older than the Pyramids, has more secrets to be exposed.

The later stage of Stonehenge construction includes the horseshoe of five great trilithons, an inner horseshoe of nineteen stones and the thirty upright stones capped with a continuous circle of lintels among other works in stone. These modifications, dated to circa-1700 to-1350 BC, are now thought to be much older constructions which, in turn, indicates a first stage of sometime much earlier than the present age of 2350. It is Stonehenge Stage 2 which intrigues me. It may be that the origins of Stonehenge go back another 1000-years

Long vanished from sight (but not from site) are stones forming parts of two concentric circles, each containing 43 holes spaced at regular intervals. And 43 is the final figure to which I reduced each individual reign from the Sumerian King-lists. Experts are in agreement that not all stones, in the new design, were placed in position. What is important is the fact that this was the original intention.

In addition to the 2x43 circles of stones were seven more as the diagram indicates. You will recall from previous chapters that 43, as a value, has lunar associations.

The following calculations are suggestions of how these circles could have served the purposes of Stonehenge mathematicians.

7 x 43 = 301.
301 x 18.604651 = 5600.
301 is also 100 x 56 (Aubrey Holes) ÷18.604651.
or, 100 x 3.01.
6 x 43 x 18.604651 = 4800.
5 x 43 x 18.604651 = 4000. And so on in steps of reduction by 800.
  This last contains much in common with the king-list calculations.

Two circles of 43 stones each, plus 7 used twice, once for each circle, gives 86 + 14 = 100.

In my examination of the Round Table legend I divide 1600 (knights/nights) by 86, (56 Aubrey Holes plus 30 Y Holes). 86 is 2 x 43. 1600 ÷ 86 = 18.604651.

The above 100 could be employed in the correction of the 3.01 Aubrey Hole anomaly: if one anticipates 5600 years into the future, it is possible that those who created that gigantic calculator envisaged some future reincarnation in human form. 56 ÷ 18.604651 = 3.01.

One may only guess as to why this particular layout of stones was finally abandoned prior to it's completion. The workforce might have gone on strike, bored with working on the flat, preferring to create something more of a grandiose monument to their capabilities. Maybe the person died, whose concept it was, an unlucky omen from which arose a taboo on the project. A change in leadership bringing fresh ideas?

There is another possibility that, assuming a conformity of change from matriarchalism to patriarchalism, male gods replacing former female goddesses, as elsewhere throughout the Continent of Europe, sun-worship replaced lunar whilst creation of the two circles was in progress, this pattern being lunar orientated.

So up went the great trilithons making up the Horseshoe, solar in inclination, a future temple to Apollo.

This supposition is far from fanciful, for there continued a perpetual trafficking of human beings throughout the whole of Europe from as far away as the Aegean, this supported by archaeological discoveries, new trends being introduced, religious or otherwise.

Apart from some axe-engravings at Stonehenge, from their weathering shown to be of ancient origins, there are dagger designs. Of these last is one which caused agitation in scholarly heads. Deeply incised into a trilithon is a dagger that bears a very close resemblance to others found only amongst late Mycenaean ruins. I do not doubt that many a learnèd archaeologist's eyebrows have hit the hairline when first espying this dagger. Nonetheless, that sole dagger engraving does lend strong support to Ireland's legendary invasions by people from the Aegean Sea vicinity.

There remains one numerical coincidence, or two to be more precise. When viewed from the centre of the Stonehenge complex, are that known as declinations of the moon, their high and low points reached by our satellite during winter months, to either side of the Heel Stone. In degrees of arc they are +29 and +19. There are 29 Z Holes and 19 stones making up the Inner Horseshoe. There are other lunar alignments to be found at Stonehenge, with declinations of -29 and -19 degrees. Unless some wizard in astronomy proves differently I will continue to treat this as pure coincidence.

I took a further look at the two circles. Since 43 provides a strong indication of a lunar association why an axis that is of a solar orientation? Was there some inbuilt factor that would link both lunar and solar aspects in the design? The Metonic cycle of nineteen years came to mind, that being equivalent of 235 lunations.

The extra seven stones are divided into groups of 1, 2 and 4. I toyed with these basic figures with a lunar inclination to the fore.
43 + 4 = 47. 47 x 2 = 94. 235 ÷ 47 = 5.
56 (Aubrey Holes) + 29 (Z Holes) + 19 (Inner- horseshoe Stones) = 94.

In the above there is a suggestion of possible, and relatively short-term, periods of calculated time, 7.6 solar years equalling 94 lunations, or 3.8 against 47 lunation's, which last, x 5, is 19 years.

The single stone might have been placed to provide half-counts, however, could it be so-positioned to provide sight-lines through the other six, giving warning stages in the moon's approach toward the end of each Metonic cycle as the orb traverses the summer solstice alignment? I am in no position to establish such a possibility. That requires the expertise of a professional astro-archaeologist.

As with other numerical values to be seen at Stonehenge I must firmly rule out any intrusion of Chance having a role in the overall design. I offer theories, and no more.

If you refer to the diagram, on a preceding page, you will notice extra stones placed across the axis, plus two which rest above the line of the circle. Positioned thus they are mindful of the positions of former posts erected across the line of the summer solstice sunrise position. I leave any possible interpretation of that to the expert.

Stonehenge Extra!

Viewed from the centre of the Stonehenge complex a full-moon would appear above the Heel Stone once in each 19 years' period.. Here again the 19-year cycle, and 19 denominators from the Sumerian King-lists calculations. This cycle is normally referred to as the Year of Meton, name of a Greek astronomer, 5th. Century BC. This lunar event occurs a few minutes after winter solstice sunset. 19 is, of course, the number of Bluestones at Stonehenge.

I here draw upon the work of Peter Lancaster Brown, a man of some standing in the field of astro-archaeology. He refers to the Diodorus legend of Hyperborea.

We are told of the god Apollo, that he visits the land of the Hyperboreans every 19 years, to appear at the circular temple where he plays music upon a citharia, (a form of lyre) and dances continuously from the vernal equinox until the rising of the Pleiades.

A number of eminent researchers have suggested varied themes, of their own, in relation to the Stonehenge/Apollo/Temple theory. Among these is Newnham who proposed that *dancing* may well be linked to the illusion created by the abnormal size that a rising harvest-moon presents. I, personally, have experienced sight of one such, a full-moon of apparent enormous and intimidating proportions, but this was just prior to a sunrise.

Peter Lancaster Brown believes that the dancing may well reflect the time when a full-moon appears to hover for long periods, close to the horizon in northern latitudes.

Some earlier investigators into Stonehenge seem to have been influenced by wishful thoughts. One Godfrey Higgins (1829-?) was convinced that the circles were of Celtic-Druid origins, and wrongly so. They are far too historically early for that. He also stated that the outer circle of stones numbered 60, the base number for cycles of antiquity. Did he also believe in a former 360-day year, as others would wish on us in order that mathematical equations can be proven? The Sumerian and Stonehenge calculations depend solely upon a sidereal year of 365.25636 days duration, as do solar alignments, at Stonehenge.

Plato's Great Year, of 36000 years, contains both king-lists divisors of 18.604651 and 43, among others, 360 being only incidental.

There is a further cycle from antiquity, that of 26000 years. Multiply this by 10 then divide by 18.604651, the answer being 13975, again possible to reduce to 43.

Higgins also saw a Stonehenge circle of 40 stones. No one else has ever done so, although he did observe, in a most roundabout manner, evidence of a Metonic cycle of 19 years in length. This he did by mental manipulation of two of his 40 stones to leave 38, which is 2 x 19. Erik von Däniken had his predecessors.

To date no Pleiades connection with Stonehenge has, to my knowledge, been exhibited. Nevertheless, Lockyear mentions 16 Pleiades alignments which he researched at other megalithic sites around Britain.

We have adopted the old Greek diminutive for the Pleiades, that of The Seven Sisters. To Australian Aborigines they represent a group of young women. To Florida Indians they are known as The Company of Sisters. To Sumerians they were The Seven Gods. It was with tongue firmly in cheek that I divided 360° by 29 (Z Holes), the answer being 12.413793, in turn multiplied by 4 to produce 49° 39.3's. Yet this figure is surprisingly close to solstice azimuths discovered by Professor Thom at Stonehenge.

Observed from the Aubrey Hole centre Thom calculated a solstice azimuth of 49° 47.3', and 49° 45.5' from the Heel Stone. Dates for these azimuths are given, respectively, as 2700 (± 400) BC and 3300

(± 400) BC. These dates are in close agreement with carbon-dating results of more recent times.

Two days ago I learnt that the Sumerian King-lists tablets date back to c.1900-1800 BC, probably copies of material from 2123-2113 BC.

Sumeria, in southern Mesopotamia, is often given title of being the first known example of civilization. However, it has become obvious that Stonehenge astronomers had reached an earlier level of intelligent modes of calculation. The latter's methods of recording information were not made upon small tablets of clay. Their's was on a much grander scale, the complete Stonehenge complex, as a lunar time calendar. To me it would seem that this required no small degree of organization on a vast scale. So just where lies the root of civilization?

So much nonsense was taught during my schooldays, with the Church's blessing.

For a short while I dwelt in the Dordogne region of France, ten-minutes car-drive from the Les Eyzies Museum of pre-history and right amongst caves where Neanderthal and Cro-Magnon people created priceless works of art,, some of which I was able to examine in situ. When these magnificent *art-galleries* and contents were first discovered, the Church denied them their rightful antiquity. Well, had not some learned man-of-the-Church already proven that man came into being only 6006 years ago, or thereabouts?

Picasso! What next?

And I was taught that pre-Roman Britons were to be likened to wild beasts with the same level of intelligence. Ancient Greeks and Egyptians were a different matter. It becomes, nonetheless, increasingly clear that Stonehenge astronomers existed prior to their Sumerian counterparts, if the above dates are acceptable proof.

Why that early fixation over lunar cycles when time could be measured by the sun? They were in need of something by which to calculate time in lesser spans for purposes of agriculture and ritual practices. Some nations made use of 'warning-stars'- Sirius to the Egyptians, the rising of the Pleiades for Greek farmers, to tell them when to plough and sow. Our own agri-industry farmers of today rip and tear the sod with careless abandon, speed the spur, seasons ignored in pursuit of maximum profit. Plough in the rest of that crop; market prices must be kept at the highest of levels! Super markets have us in their power!

The Sarsen Circle.
Thirty Gates to Knowledge.

The Sarsen Circle was a masterpiece of engineering, its pillars placed precisely in position, lintels mortised to fit upon their tops, and mortised to join end-to-end, one with another. Un-jointed pyramid blocks would be easy to align, a few taps here and there with mallets, a straightedge of stretched rope sufficient a guide, no curving line to follow.

Those mortise and tenon joints had to be prepared in advance with no possibility of pre-erection tests. Not so many years ago they re-built Birmingham's New Street Station employing slabs of pre-stressed concrete. Some of those slabs were squared to form a lift-well. From floor-level to level they did not align, regardless of the modern techniques then available to engineers.

At Stonehenge they must have possessed some form of measure, crude plum-bobs, ropes and levers, antlers their picks and shovels, flints and stone-mauls their shaping tools.

So how did they create such a marvel? Did they build an advance mock-up in timber?

The most difficult of tasks would be the raising of pillars, the lifting into position of the lintel-stones presenting even greater problems, those mortise-joints permitting no leeway for error, particularly so in the forming of a circle. It required quite literally years before I discovered a numerical key to the Sumerian King-lists enigma. The same applies to this, the erection of the Sarsen Circle, for I considered that there might exist a method that would be less open to error, accidental breaking of human bone, with the present theory of how the lintel- stones were lifted up, a somewhat hazardous method.

De Bono gives the expression, Lateral Thinking. So I literally laterally thought. I thought down, not up!

Well why didn't I think of that? You said that. On occasion I have said the same.

My theory called for a suitable mechanism whereby gravity would provide the major force used in opposition to conventional ideas on the subject.

With care one digs holes to the required depth, each hole placed precisely, one to the next, upon the circumference of a circle. Against the inner wall of the hole, a tall pole is erected in a vertical position. This is for later location of each hole's position..

Stage One:

Build a mound of easily-compacted chalky substance, a mound, as in diagrams to follow, with vertical sides bordering the holes' inner sides. To the mounds add ramps of the same material, with a gentle gradient. Slot lengths of timber into Ramp One in the fashion of railway lines. At the top of the second ramp fix an A-frame, suited to hinging at the base. Tie long ropes to the top of the A-frame, reaching Ramp One's base for tying to a lintel-stone by members of the work-force. Each pull on those ropes would move the lintel-stone up it's ramp in stages, each stage governed by the arc through which the A-frame top moves, a descending arc that would, because of the in-built geometry, not be worth pulling to the horizontal. There would be animal fats available for the greasing of the *Railway-lines*..

Stage Two:

With all 60 stones resting on top of the mound, remove the A—frame, Remove some of the ramp material, as depicted in following figure, the vertical timbers a guide to where the pillar holes are positioned. Now slide the first pillar-stone down ward, guiding it into it's hole with ropes and levers. Tamp it to remain firm and upright. Proceed with the remaining pillars.

In similar fashion lower the lintels into positions.

Stage Three.

Ramp and mound spoil is removed for scattering elsewhere, to leave the original surface as it was prior to commencement of building construction. Such an operation would leave no clue to how the task was carried out.

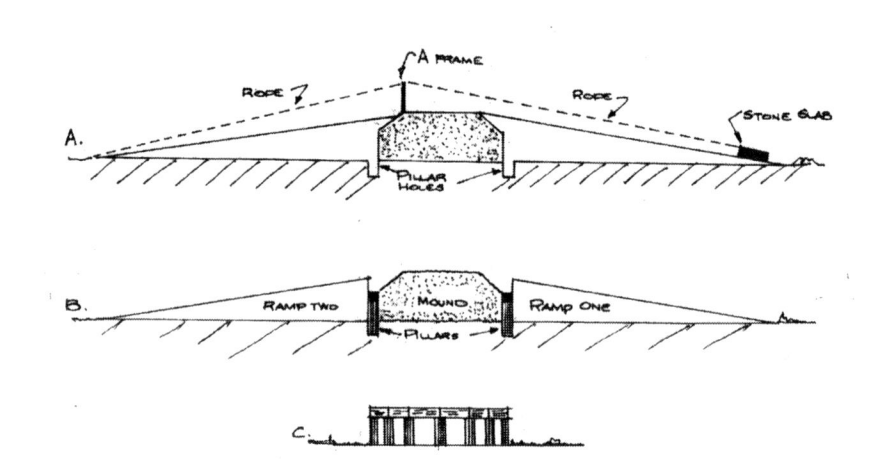

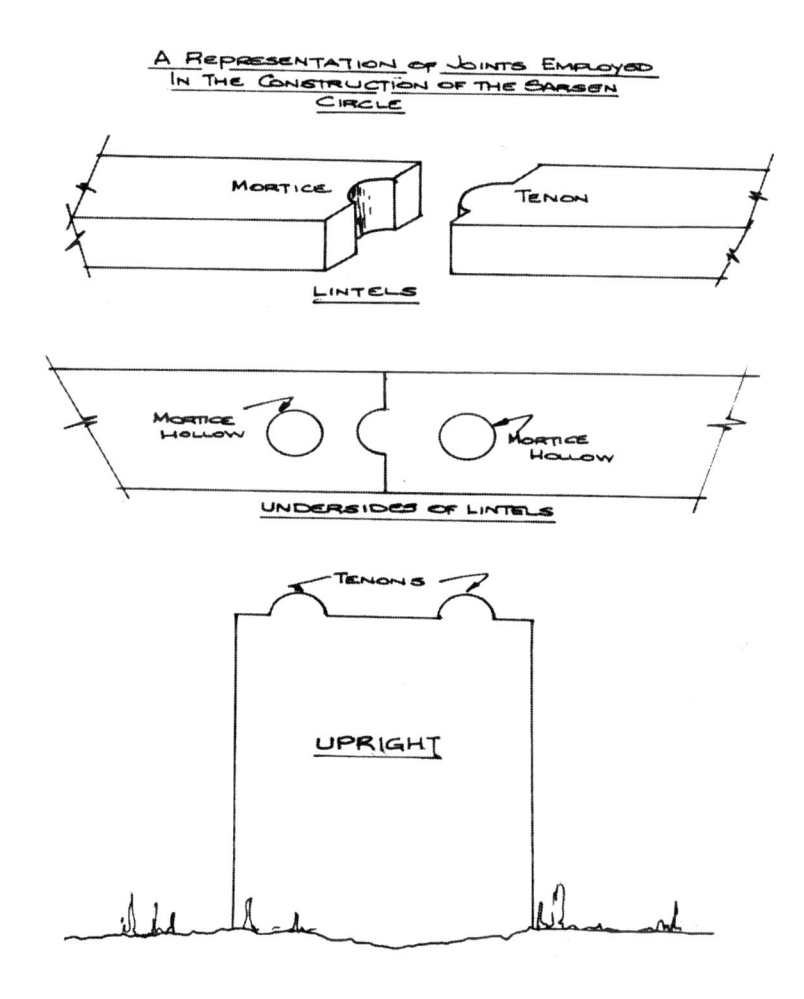

A REPRESENTATION OF JOINTS EMPLOYED IN THE CONSTRUCTION OF THE SARSEN CIRCLE

MORTICE TENON

LINTELS

MORTICE HOLLOW   MORTICE HOLLOW

UNDERSIDES OF LINTELS

TENONS

UPRIGHT

Q.E.D. With expenditure of a lot less sweat.

I hope that, in my layman's fashion, I have convinced you of the importance of lunar over solar, female over male, aspect of Stonehenge before it became a temple to Apollo.

The metonic cycle of 19 years equals almost precisely 235 lunations. Others have demonstrated the following.

Assuming the outer circle of stones to be 59 in number, it might possibly be 60 or 61-add together all numerical values to be found at Stonehenge....

19-10-59-30-29-30- 1 (Heel Stone) - 56 to equal 235.

Now you know why Stonehenge astronomers dug seemingly useless holes. They knew a thing or two, did they, about moonlight, not, as some would claim,moonshine.

The Eight Year Venus Cycle.

The Ancients were aware of the Venus Cycle, that period of years when the planet reached it's apogees, it's five furthermost points in the sky as seen from Earth, five points which form those of a perfect pentagram. All angles, formed by a pentagram, are in multiples of 18°s.

One of the divisors that I applied to the Sumerian King-lists, is that of 360 which is the number of divisions normally associated with a circle, in degrees-value. I wondered were there signs, in the king- lists, suggestive of the Venus-cycle factor? This required employment of the figure 18. I had doubts that figures, precisely divisible by 18.604651 could also be similarly divisible by 18, for obvious reasons.

Table 4.

Reign Number	Length of	Div 18.60451	Div 18.0
1	28800	1548	1600
2	36000	1935	2000
3	64800	3483	3600
4	43200	2322	2400
5	21000	1128.75	1166.666
6	18600	999.75	1033.333
7	241200	12964.5	13400
8	36000	1935	2000
9	108000	5805	6000
10	28000	1505	1555.555

The results showed promise but, yet again, there were oddities. If I added together reigns 5 and 6 they would total 39600 which, divided by 18 gives 2200. As on the earlier occasion I also added reigns 5, 6 and 7 to present a total of 280800. This figure, too, is exactly divisible by 18; answer 15600.

Take that 15600 and subtract from it the Reigns 5, 6 and 7 companion figures in the third column-1128.75 + 999.75 + 12964.5 = 15093; 15600 -15093 = 507.

By sub-division-507 ÷ (13 x 13) = 3.

Strange to say, the three companion quantities in Column 4 add up to 15599.999. I think that you will accept this as 15600.

With the exception of reign 10 the figure 13 can be likewise applied.

Reign 9; 6000 – 5805 = 195.

195 ÷ 13 = 15.which is easily reduced to 3, or 5.

Reign 1; 1600 – 1548 = 52 = 13 x 4.

Reign number 10 presents a problem as yet unsolved.

From the Aegean came a calendar to Ireland via Spain. It was the Beth Luis Nion calendar with a year of 13 months, each month of 28 days duration,,, with one day in a sort of limbo. The calendar commenced with the winter solstice when, once upon a time, the sacred king would have been sacrificed as was Actaeon to Artemis on that day, when one reads between the lines, or beneath the obscuring skin of old myth. Could this explain the origins of unlucky thirteen, for that solstice brought the end of the thirteenth month in the Beth Luis Nion calendar.

A representation of the Beth Luis Nion Tree-Calendar.

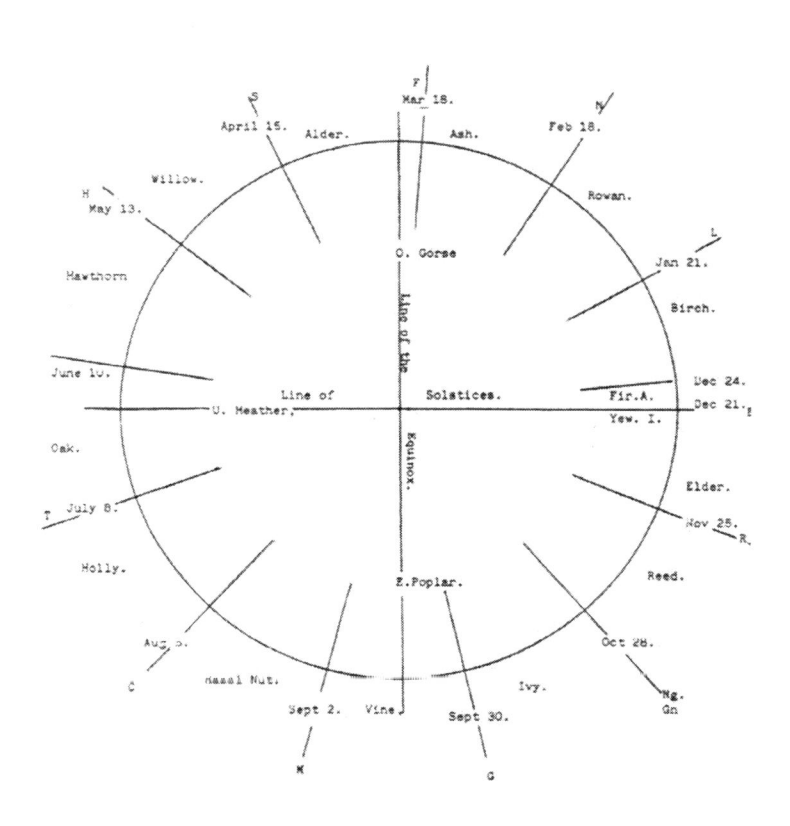

The Gods of Stonehenge?

I here state, with no prevarication, that Alford's Thoth, nor any other of his gods, was ever present to teach human beings some rather advanced techniques in matters of astronomy and the creation of associated observatories.

Prior to the first digging of a hole at Stonehenge, the tribe's astronomers must have spent many decades, hundreds of years the probability, in the making of some type of record, perhaps memorized and passed on down from generation to generation, as was common among original Bards. Druid apprentices spent years in becoming word-perfect in the knowledge taught, for instance. At Stonehenge this may have involved the putting to memory a few essential figures, simple and possibly as few as four in number.

For me the queen of all constructions at Stonehenge is the Sarsen Circle. Yet, as I shall demonstrate, those seemingly insignificant holes at the site are grouped so as to serve explicit purposes. Of these are the two concentric circles of holes, the Q and R, intended to have a stone placed in each, the project never completed. It might have been that that so grand a sight would be too ostentatious, the holes alone sufficient for the purpose. Although the erection of the Sarsen Circle might belie the theory.

Greeks, when making mention of a circular temple, to the north, had every right to wonder, for in lands around such edifices were all *built on the square.* Even pyramid-builders would marvel at the precision embodied within construction of the Sarsen Circle.

Sir Norman Lockyear, in 1931, confirmed William Stukeley's earlier discovery that the henge was aligned with sunrise at the summer-solstice. In the wake of this others have searched for other important alignments, in the Stonehenge complex. Professor of Engineering,

Alexander Thom, carried out that which is perhaps the best in-situ survey at the site, to observe that it contains built-in facilities for observing lunar as well as solar cycles. He also pointed out that had the henge been constructed a mile or two away in any direction, then it can never have performed that which was required of it.

Who constituted the World's first astronomers? I propose that shepherds, guarding their flocks by night, to be the likeliest contenders for that title .They, better-placed than anyone, would have plenty of time to watch the night-skies, and wonder. Doubtless they would 'compare notes' with fellow shepherds and take note of repetitive cycles in both moon and sun and other of our planets. They would notice positions of moon and sun sets and rises at positions which changed, month by month, upon the horizons. And, with a responsibility to maintain the size of the flock, he-she would be called upon to keep a count of it's numbers.

If the criteria governing what constitutes a civilization, is an ability to organize, possess numeracy, plan in advance, and construct in stone then, as with the Sumerians, the people of Stonehenge formed a civilization. And like both the Sumerians and Egyptians they appear out of nowhere. But no advanced civilisation ever arrived *ready-made*. I suggest that wandering tribes, herders of flocks, commenced to remain awhile at some fertile spot, there they farmed the land until it lost its fertility. They then moved on to seek another area of green which, in like fashion, was farmed until it became barren.

Came the day that the wandering tribe reached it's Garden of Eden, land to either side of a broad river whose annual floods kept the soil perpetually verdant with food for all, without fear of starvation. They no longer had need of portable shelters with so much clay at hand. They no longer had need to drive flocks up mountain sides for summer pasture.

During former travels their ancestors acquired knowledge that was handed on for the benefit of future generations. In a permanent settlement, as they now were, they could rest and make use of that knowledge, even going so far as to build structures in stone, their Temple and Observatory. Well-fed, tribal numbers would increase, the Elders in control of religious ceremonies arranging sacrifices to the deities who had given them a life of plenty. Their itinerant mode of life a thing of the past, those people can now devote themselves to a rapid conversion to a stabilized way of life, blossoming into an organized society within a matter of a few decades. They had no need of gods to instruct them.

Constructors of Stonehenge would seem to have arrived out of the blue, to employ modern ,jargon, with a ready knowledge of cycles of time as applies to both moon and sun. This knowledge they wished to record with permanence of a visible nature, and in such a manner that future initiates shall recognize and put to use the facility. It would enable them to predict, well in advance, the next lunar-standstill for they were more concerned with the moon than the sun. For the moon to arrest itself would be a day of great wonder, perhaps one of terror, the gods to be placated in order that the silver orb shall not fall upon their heads.

A Stonehenge and Hyperborean Re-appraisal.

Some later stages, in Stonehenge construction, can be dated from nearby barrows containing chipping from the same stones.

From those barrows a large number of grave-goods have been unearthed, beautifully-wrought ornaments of intricate workmanship. They include beads in faience and amber, gold-plated buttons, gold cups, amber discs and necklaces, all bearing the stamp of Mycenaean work. Those finds give credence to the dagger-carvings on Stone number 53 at Stonehenge, daggers thought to be of Mycenaean design, suggestive of a date about 1470 BC.

That date throws the Mycenaean theory in conflict with grave-goods dated to the Wessex Culture to which they belong. That is due to a Wessex Culture thought to be from 2100-1700 BC, whereas the Mycenaean equivalent is dated from 1600 BC.

But later radio-carbon dating now places the ending of the Wessex Culture to around 1500 BC. when making allowances to either side of 1500 and 1470 BC, they may easily bring an overlap.

The history of Stonehenge is to be seen in stages of construction which I now proceed to delineate.

Stage 1; 3190 - 2300 BC.
    The digging of Ditch and Bank with gap to north east.
    The Cursus.
    The 56 Aubrey Holes.
Stage 2; 2150- 2000 BC.
    The axis of the site is deliberately modified by a slight degree, which may have been carried out in order to give a more-refined accuracy in observation of the sun's horizonal position at the summer solstice.
    Also included with this stage are the incompleted, concentric circles

of Bluestones, the Q and R Stones, 43 to each circle.

It is proposed that the re-orientation of the axis is linked with sun- worship. I doubt this, for my calculations indicate a lunar bias for important observations at the site. This does,, however, necessitate comparisons with solar-time.

Stage 3A; 2150—2000 BC.

The circle of 30 upright, lintelled stones is incorporated into the complex. 30 is one of my lunar figures. This is the Sarsen Circle.

From the remaining stones the Sarsen Circle depicts work of a master-craftsman, in expertize shown in the lintel jointing, and the manner in which continuity of line is presented by the lintels, fashioned smooth and curving upon both inner and outer faces to create a perfect circle overhead.

That expertize is continued in interlocking mortise and tenon joints which stabilise the positions of lintels upon upright stones.

Whoever designed those joints was most certainly someone well-practised in the art of *heavy-construction*, a Mycenaean perhaps, a craftsman who learnt his trade in similar projects back in Greece? The same type of jointing is to be found in the Mycenaean Postern Gate.

This stage includes the setting up of the Trilithon Horseshoe of ten uprights with five lintels.

Stage 3B; 2060-1550 BC.

Nineteen stones of the Inner Horseshoe are placed in position. Toward the end of this period Y and Z holes are excavated. We now have all that is required to duplicate the king-list divisor values.

Stage 3C;   2000-1550 BC.

Y and Z Holes are refilled.

Each of the above stages appear to have been manufactured to improve facilities in the making of astronomical observations, all primarily lunar-associated, according to my mathematics.

I sought far and wide, through relevant texts,, in search of at least one other round-temple, worthy of a god, among ancient cultures.

Constructions, of importance to persons of high rank, or sacred to prevailing deities, were all built *on the square,* with squared corners and roofed-over high walls. Ziggurats and pyramids follow the same pattern. Much later, within the bounds of Greece proper, and invaded territories, sacred temples continue to be influenced by that on-the-square formula with temple architecture, bases always rectangular, roofs supported by Ionic and other styles of columns to protect sacred, inner sanctums.

The circular temple of the Hyperboreans receives attention through the pens of Diodorus and company, and no other such magnificent structure. Had another existed surely they would have made record of such a wonder, a rarity in their contemporary world.

I made earlier mention of Pytheas of Massilia, he who circumnavigated Old Albion, circa 300 BC. Pytheas left behind a record in which he describes the inhabitants of Britain, and a climate that he, from warmer climes, found to be extremely cold. He also made note of the fact that Britain lies beneath the constellation of the Great Bear. He is telling, of course, of a country to which came his distant forebears.

Hecataeus describes a large island, lying to the north of Gaul, where live the Hyperboreans, so named because they live beyond the point from which Boreas, the North Wind blows, a fertile land, too.

And Hecataeus, courtesy of Diodorus, tells of one Hyperborean, Arabis, who makes an exchange visit to Greece after Greeks had come to the Land of the Hyperboreans bearing costly gifts, some of which are inscribed with letters of the Greek alphabet. Aha, think I, maybe this will blow the British-Hyperborean hypothesis wide apart. I went in search of early alphabets.

The Phoenicians introduced their alphabet, containing no vowels, about 1700 BC among the nation's inventions. It was Greeks who added the vowels for the alphabet upon which our own is rooted.

With a Wessex/Hyperborean overlap of cultures appearing to be a reality the Greek gifts bearing letters of an expanded vowelled-alphabet, becomes a possibility.

I previously proposed that the two pairs of Hyperborean maidens, en route to the Isle of Delos, might have travelled via the south coast of France, thence around Italy, in like fashion, to cross the Adriatic, to the island of Corfu from where it would be a short passage by water to the Greek mainland and nearby Dodona. Hyperborean Arabis is said to have journied eastward to reach the northern coast of the Adriatic, when he wished to visit Delos, moving via Dodona. This seems to be a reversal of the route that I suggested for the girls. It might be seen to imply a different location for the Land of the Hyperboreans. A look at a map of Europe gives the answer.

Robert Graves, when tracing voyages made by the Argonauts, makes mention of the River Danube, probably the oldest, long-distance trading route on the Continent.

Arabis would have left his homeland-Britain intent upon reaching the Rhine, up which he would travel to come within a comfortable walking distance of the upper reaches of the Danube.

That great waterway runs to south-east prior to sweeping to east and the Black Sea. However, before reaching that bend, he would find a suitable river that would take him to general west and the northern Adriatic from where to follow the coast down to Dodona, an important centre for pilgrimages. They did have boats, those travellers of yore. And ferry-men. It was along the Danube that Greeks travelled in search of Baltic amber. Are those Wessex amber beads made from Baltic material?

I have a better homeland for the Sons of Milen, mentioned in the Irish Invasions saga. It is the island of Milos in the Aegean Cyclades, much nearer to volcanic Thera than is Crete. And Thera might have been the direct cause why the Sons of Milen decided to move far from homes which had been undergoing far too many a shaking of walls and roof from around 1600 BC, onwards until mad old Zeus brought Thera to blow her hollow top with all of the power that he could muster. Maybe, up around Albion-way, effusions of crazed Zeus' wrath would be less potent. So the Sons of Milen, islanders and seamen, set sail to the west.

Stonehenge astronomers dug their 56 Aubrey Holes. And they found errors creeping into their calculations, a problem for future generations to solve. And thus someone saw fit to erect two circles of stones, numbering 43 to each circle. Who can say why the project was abandoned? The holes required would suffice for purposes of lunar-associated calculation.

With or without the stones in place they knew the secret of the gods. They could measure the cycles, the years ordained by Sky Mother and Sky Father, respectively dwelling on the moon and sun. Big Magic!

But surely Sky Mother and Sky Father deserved a more grandiose style of temple, one that would incorporate the secrets of time-observance. Sacred beings warranted the expenditure of so much time and sweat.

We will devise a great edifice in stone that contains even more powerful magic, for our children's children, and their children's children to complete after our spirits are set finally free to observe so magnificent a project from our place high in the skies, lords of all that we survey.

Please forgive the flight of fancy! Yet surely those creators of Stonehenge would have their dreams, their visions of the greatest of temples ever. When arriving on the scene Apollo would be delighted with what he saw,, long after they were gone.

Where else lies an island, to north of Gaul, that in ancient times Abaris left en route to paying a visit the Delians?

In conclusion the following -

> It is long since I was a herdsman.
> I travelled over the Earth
> before I became a learned person.
> I have travelled; I have made a circuit;
> I have slept in a hundred islands;
> I have dwelt in a hundred cities. Learned Druids,
> prophesy ye of Arthur?
> Or is it me they celebrate?

Gwion, with whom this passage is associated, seems to be a mythical character whose birth and childhood have magical qualities, some of them paralleled in Greek mythology.

Young Gwion set to stir the contents of Cerridwen's magic cauldron, three drops from which fall upon the lad's finger that he sucks and immediately understands the meaning of all things. The brew also gives him the ability to shape-shift into other forms of life. Cerridwen's cauldron had properties like those of Greek Medea whose vessel had the qualities of re-birth and inspiration. Gwion was renamed Taleisin I.

Apollo must be the 'I' in the above passage. He was formerly a herdsman. As a pre-Greek oracular hero he had 'rested in a Hundred Sacred Islands. After Greeks adopted Cretan Apollo, as their God of Healing and Music, he became sun-god with daily *Circuits* as represented by the sun.

When Druids prophesy of Arthur, one assumes that this refers to his second-coming. But all heroes have their second-comings. They are sacrificed and are re-born in Paradises of Immortality, their Avalons or Lands of the Blessed, or on Earth in the form of a 'Twin'.

Hecateus wrote of a temple, sacred to Apollo. That temple, of the Hyperboreans, must be Stonehenge previously dedicated to the Triple Goddess, and lunar when Matriarchal rule applied.

By virtue of his name Arthur has connections with the Bear. And so did Apollo by indirect association.

In Minoan Crete the Goddess ruled unchallenged. Of her daughters was Artemis. Apollo, at that time, was an inferior because of his masculinity. Apollo was twin of an Artemis famed and worshipped in Arcadia and the Ardennes Forest, where her totem-animal was the Bear,,, in the sense that, promoted above Artemis to sun-god, Apollo, as her twin, cannot escape taking on the Goddess's mantle along with it's accompanying Bear.

An hypothesis, another one...

We have a Guinevere in triplicate, doubling for the lunar triad with her three-fold dis-appearances and re-appearances, She is Lady-of-the-Lake Artemis in Maiden aspect, she Of the Three Ways, White and accompanied by a Bear. And Guinevere, mysterious lady, has the power to lead Arthur quite a dance to suit her own unpredictable designs. It is my questionable theory that Guinevere is the Lunar Goddess, Arthur her king to be sacrificed to her, all else mere decorative embellishment.

The Quest: Arthur's band of merry men had lost account of time, of days and nights. There was, however, a secret formula whereby the error could be rectified. It lay at Stonehenge in the numerical values of its circles. This then was the Grail.

The word, Grail, reminds me of a Grid or Grill, an heraldic Gate.

At Stonehenge lay the Gate to Knowledge, such as that conferred upon Gwion/Taleisin. The Grail had yet to be made Holy, at some 500 years BC.

When Apollo/Arthur became equated with patriarchal dominance over earlier matriarchalism, and of sun-worship over lunar obeisance, there arose a problem.

So insistent were they upon observation of a solar calendar that they lost sight of it's lunar equivalent. They had to recapture the magic of a secret tree-alphabet that the Irish and Welsh had imported from the Aegean. It was the Beth Luis Nion alphabet/calendar.

Imagine the confusion of a priesthood, suddenly confronted with a takeover from ruling priestesses with millenia of experience with the tree-calendar, now abruptly become solar orientated, proud female counterparts quite rightly refusing to assist in the transition.

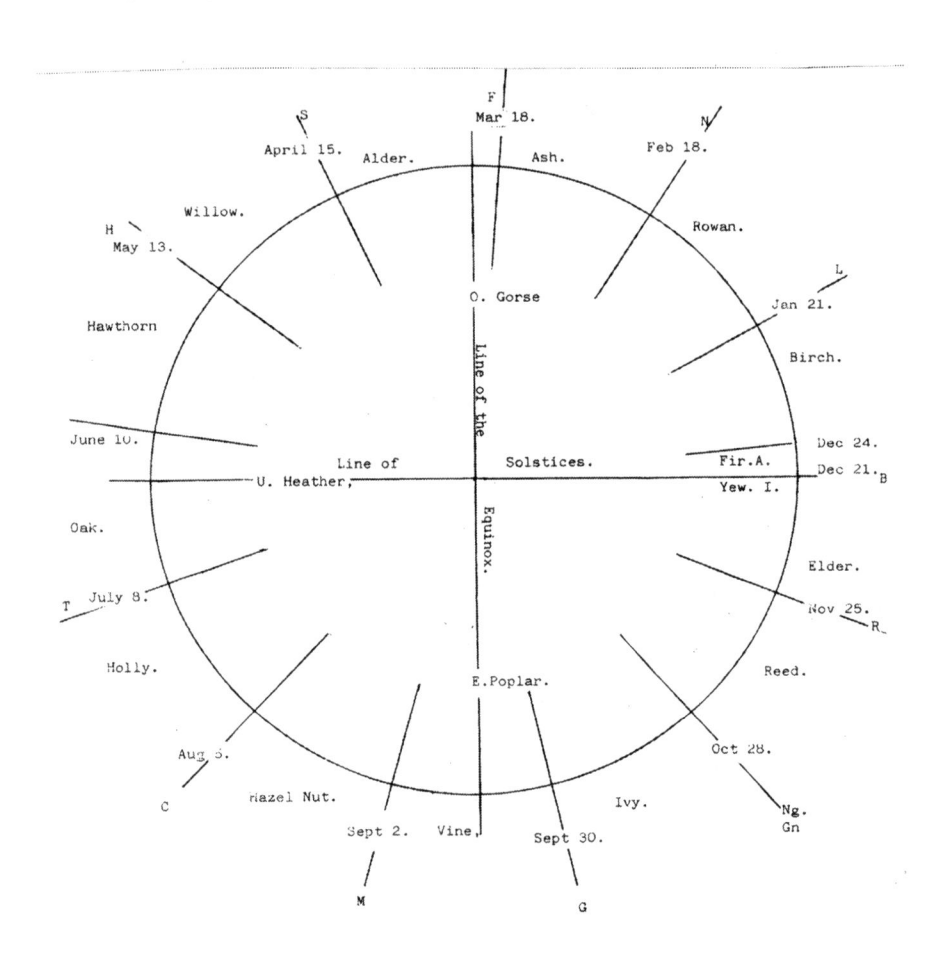

The Beth Luis Nion tree-calendar.

Ignore Russell Grant and associate star-gazers! Here is your opportunity to add the thirteenth sign, Ophiucus the Serpent Holder. between Reed and Elder, Scorpio and Sagittarius. So I, a Taurian, am not that which present-day *horrorscopologists* would suggest. Old Moores Almanac is in dire need of revision.

The Beth Luis Nion Tree Calendar of 13 months duration:

Each month has its particular Tree, each Tree having its own magical qualities.

I discovered all of the associated qualities within the pages of Robert Graves, beautifully annotated, The Greek Myths in two volumes. I commence at December the 24th. with it's equivalent tree.

24th. December: Birch: Expeller of evil influences.   Letter B.

21st. January. Rowan.   Letter L.

18th. February: Ash: Rain and Fire-making. Lunar- association.
   Letter N.

18th. March: Alder: Associated with Witch-goddess *Circe*.   Letter F.

15th. April: Willow: Rain-making.   Letter S.

13th. May: Hawthorn; Tree of Earth Goddess.   Letter H.

10th. June: Oak· Fire, Rain, and Lightning affiliations.   Letter D.

8th. July: Holly.   Letter T.

5th. August: Nut (Hazel?) Wisdom.   Letter C.

2nd. September: Vine?   Letter M.

30th. September: Ivy: Provides ceremonial red dye. Symbolic of the Earth-goddess. Is an intoxicant with creative powers.   Letter G.

28th. October: Reed. ?   Letter Gn

25th. November: Elder. ?   Letter R.

Winter Solstice. Fir and Yew: Death.   Letters A and I.

Spring Equinox: Gorse.   Letter 0.

Summer Solstice: Heather.   Letter U.

Autumn Equinox: Poplar.   Letter E.

    The figure above depicts my endeavours to reconstruct a Beth Luis Nion calendar from information contained within Graves' The Greek Myths. You will notice that vowels coincide with both equinox and solstice points, A and I sharing the winter solstice line, with associated trees. This is a thirteen consonant/five vowel alphabet, later to be replaced by the extended Boibel Loth counterpart. Although individual trees possess occult secrets, more spiritual in meaning, there are cases of replacement trees in the latter.

    The dates, that I include, are today's equivalents, for this calendar is far-older than any Julian of Gregorian equivalent by more than a millennium.

    For those who may wish to know more on the subject I suggest Graves' The White Goddess wherein the author goes into great detail concerning both Beth Luis Nion and Boibel Loth calendars, also providing surprising parallels between Greek and Irish alphabet, in the names for individual letters.

An Extension of the Hyperborean Legend.

Further investigation into the works of Diodorus Siculus, 1st century BC, reveals that his description of the Land of the Hyperboreans is based, in part, upon a voyage undertaken by Pytheas of Massilia who carried out a circumnavigation of the British Isles about 300 BC. At that date Greeks had long been taking copper and tin from Cornwall, and amber from the Baltic coasts to their homeland by land, river and sea.

The Greek writer, Herodotus, who lived at approximately the same time as Hecateus (his writings no longer extant), known to us as the Father of History, fifth century BC, is another upon whom Diodorus drew when compiling his own work of a literary nature.

Treating his work as being historical fact Herodotus tells of Hyperboreans who sent gifts to peoples of the Aegean, moving via Dodona then southward to cross over to the Isle of Euboea, thence in stages to the Isle of Delos. He introduces two maidens by name, they who accompanied the gifts. They are Hyperoche and Laodice, both of whom remained and died on the isle.

So deeply did the Delians respect the Hyperborean girls they built a tomb for them which, highly-significantly, was located by the entrance to a temple to Artemis, goddess and twin-sister to Apollo.

It is interesting to note that anyone whose tomb is set adjacent to a temple, of so powerful a goddess, could not have been more greatly revered. To show such esteem to a pair of foreign visitors would be indeed exceptional.

Another pair of Hyperborean girls had earlier made the same journey to Delos at, strangely enough, a time when Artemis and Apollo were not long introduced to the People of Delos. They, Arge and Opis, were also reverenced by the Delians, a pair of maidens who are named in a hymn written in their memory. That the names of those four girls came to be recorded at Delos, alone reveals just how much importance was placed upon them. Because of this I suggest that all four had some close religious association with Artemis.

Diodorus writes of Leto, mother of Apollo (brother of Artemis) and of Hyperborean worship of the god, his omission of Artemis due surely to a more recent turn to solar worship rather than the former lunar-directed worship, goddesses relegated under a system of patriarchal rule. It is this same Leto who promises the Delians that she will cause to be built a temple to Apollo, her son, on condition that they feed pilgrims paying homage to the god, people arriving from distant shores.

A hymn to Apollo dubs him 'Far-shooting god of the Silver Bow'. But Artemis, prior to this, is known for the Silver Bow that she sported, at a time when Apollo was her inferior. Her silver bow represented a waxing crescent moon, very appropriate for Artemis in Virgin-Maiden form, the first element of the Triple Goddess. We again have evidence to show Apollo adopting his 'big' sister's mantle.

The general usurpation of matriarchal rule by that of patriarchal, was a far from abrupt conversion, from the Middle East all across Europe. In defiance of a newly-created pantheon of gods, with Wildman Zeus in charge, goddess-worship lingered on in places right into the Christian era.

Throughout Palestine archaeological investigators have uncovered much that relates directly to goddess-worship. Much in the Old Testament is a reflection of an enforced transition from female ascendancy to that of male. The name EVE is derived from Hebrew Hirwa, itself firmly rooted in the Hittite goddess, Herwa.

The Trilithon Horseshoe at Stonehenge is now dated to 1500 BC., a little later than previous figures. Aegean peoples, according to Irish legend, commenced to arrive in Ireland around the middle of the third millenium BC. They were followed by the Pelasgians from the same Mediterranean vicinity. Then came tribes from Thrace, persuaded by the earlier settlers to move on into Scotland. At approximately 1250 BC., Miletians arrived, claiming to be descendents of Apollo. The Cretan city of Miletis is one of favoured birthplaces of Artemis/ Britomartis, and Apollo, naturally. These invaders are said to have come westward through the Mediterranean Sea via Greek Gades, today's Spanish Cadiz.

Those newcomers would have brought cultural changes to Ireland and to Britain, doubtless with emphasis upon new gods to worship. I estimate that the revised tree-alphabet, the Boibel Loth version, would have reached Ireland around 1000 BC. and, with it, more Aegean influence on cultural changes. I also propose that this was a part of continuous social changes from a much earlier date.

Between 1530 and 1470 BC. The Isle of Thera literally blew her top, ripped apart by devastating forces of Nature, following which Minoan influence in the Aegean commenced to fade. Then came the Mycenaean invasion of Crete, some of the island's population most likely fleeing from the newcomers using remnants of the Cretan fleet to move on to other lands. From whence did ancient examples of the Cretan maze, in England, come? And does that vibrantly-male chalk figure represent Heracles rather than Cernennos? Heracles did possess a huge club, too.

Greeks made Leto to be daughter of the Titans, Coeus and Phoebe and mother of Apollo and Artemis by Zeus, a further example of the male made superior to the female. But they did give the birthplace of Apollo and Artemis as being the Isle of Delos. Numerous functions, previously the arts of a variety of goddesses, are all attributed to Apollo, even as leader of the Muses, they being female, of course,

> Hark, hark the lark
> At Heaven's gate sings,
> And Phoebus 'gins arise,
> His steeds to water.....

Phoebus 'The Shining One: could this refer to, Apollo as Sun-god.? That verse ends with 'My Lady sweet arise'. I wonder could it be a discreet reference to a lunar-goddess?

What then of Diodorus with two descriptions of Hyperborean climatic conditions, one suited to the raising of two crops per year, the other one decidedly cooler?

Today a rise or fall in average annual temperature produces far greater changes in Nature than one might expect, should one heed only television weather-forecasts. Far back, during a pre-historic past, the average temperature for July in Britain was 2°C higher than today. Then, around 1500BC, lasting until 300BC, came centuries of much cooler weather.

With a July average of 6-8°C difference between Britain and Greece, the pre-historic traveller, then, coming from the Aegean to our south-west, would not have found climatic fluctuations to be so noticeable as it would be for some Thomson's tourists bound for the Island of Corfu, today.

Herodotus, through the pen of Diodorus, reveals that, commencing about the same general decline in climatic conditions throughout Europe.1500 BC, Crete became uninhabited due to pestilence and famine.

The Mycenaean culture, after spreading to mainland Greece, lasted some five centuries, from 1600-1100 BC. There is that engraving upon one of the Stonehenge trilithon uprights, said to be representative of a Mycenaean dagger.

In order to preserve their good names historians of pre-history are cautious to an extreme when referring to Greek writers of Old, even though Schliemann proved Homer to be quoting fact faithfully passed on through generations by word of mouth. If Druid apprentices spent years in a meticulous memorizing of verbal texts why should early Greeks not have done the same? Heinrich Schliemann also unearthed many Mycenaean centres of importance after intensive studies of the work of Homer who preceded Herodotus, therefore Diodorus by centuries.

The Sons of Milen, the Miletians who arrived in Ireland about 1250 BC, may well have been Mycenaean invaders of Crete, they who claimed descendancy from Apollo, Stonehenge already completed, a grandiose temple open to the skies, a place worthy of Apollo himself as Sun-god.

Have archaeological experts got it wrong?

Sources come into conflict in the dating of pre-historic cultures. There is frequent agreement for many a decade until some bright spark comes along with a theory that ignores conventional dating from ancient artefacts, grave goods, pottery jewelry and all of those other bits and pieces brought to light by much patient scraping and sieving for months on end, each tiny fragment given a thorough inspection, catalogued and brought with loving care to rest inside controlled atmospheres of world museums.

We now find the Minoan Empire commencing to crumble much earlier than suspected should one accept more recent evidence that has nothing in common with an archaeologist's faithful trowel.

Following volcanic eruptions of immense power, such as that of Krakatoa, resultant muck and ash flung miles high into the atmosphere to spread around the planet and reduce sunlight by a noticeable degree, tree-rings are affected until that ash no longer weakens the sun's light. So now Thera, with a far greater output of generated power than Krakatoa, gave a magnificent display of molten rage in the year 1628 BC, so they claim.

The Hyperborean girls, en route to the Isle of Delos, came via mainland Dodona, thence through the Isle of Euboea to come to rest within seventy miles of darling Thera. This indicates a route taken from the north-west. I drew a line through the three named places in Greece, across Europe. It hit the south-west vicinity of England, it so occurred.

Greeks placed Hyperborea to their general north, not in Macedonia nor Thrace, but somewhere far more distant. A look at a map will show that anyone coming to Greece from the north, to reach Euboea would not take a diversion to go through Dodona, not if important emissaries wishing to get from A to B by the quickest route, such as might the Hyperborean maidens, girls with no time to waste upon trips to take a look at the equivalent of an Anne Hathaway's cottage.

Dodona lay a little inland from the then coast of Greece on the Adriatic Sea. It was to east of Corfu. To the west, across a narrow strait, lay the southern tip of Italy. The Hyperborean delegates, had they come from Britain, would have a comfortable route to follow by crossing the Channel, heading south to Marseille, turn to east through Nice and on into Italy along that country's western coast.

Nevertheless, Dodona is mentioned in the Illiad, as a sanctuary to Zeus. There are strong indications that this same sanctuary was once a venue of Earth-goddess worship. There was also the Dodona Oracle where oracular messages were devised from the rustling of leaves in a grove of trees. Herodotus writes of priestesses who were diviners of such foretellings of future events. He also describes a large gong in bronze, set to vibrate by scourges held in the hand of a figure holding up the gong, the arrangement dependent upon breezes to motivate it.

I cannot prove that Stonehenge became a temple for the worship of Apollo but Britain, climatically, fits the Diodorus, account, having been warmer than today, followed by some centuries of far cooler weather.

As to that mention of two crops per year one must make allowances for the fact that, until more recent times, all crops followed normal cycles, the seed programmed by Nature to bear fruit at whichever season suited it's growth-pattern. No-one can force grain to crop twice in one year, nor an apple tree to similarly double it's output under normal conditions. There is, however, one thing that can produce two crops per annum; it is grass turned to hay.

By the ninth century BC Greeks had established colonies at Nice and Marseille on the French Mediterranean coast, a common practice once trade-routes had been created.

When my map-search for pre-historic alignments uncovered a rectangle with sides in proportion of 3 and 4, and with diagonals with 5 of the same units of measure, I suggested that so precise a survey might be the work of ancient Greeks. And, furthermore, there is also the four-cemetery alignment equivalent of sunset at the winter solstice for a calculated date of between 1000 and 400 BC.

There does exist some archaeological evidence for a Greek presence in the French Languedoc that is hardly touched by the trowel of serious investigators into the past. At Alet, to north of Rennes le Château, is an old temple (to Isis says one quite extravagant claim). The Romans, like the later Church of Rome, had a fondness for appropriating the sacred places of others to their own ends. Could that temple be Grecian?

It was within the pages of a BBC publication, The Birth of Europe that I came across a map showing early trade and exploratory routes taken by Greeks across Europe. Old, migratory and trade routes invariably followed guaranteed sources of water, like major river courses, this includes the Greeks whose sea routes encompassed the whole of the Mediterranean, venturing outside the 'Pillars of Heracles' into the Atlantic Ocean, northwards round Portugal, across the Bay of Biscay and on to reach south-western England with it's sources of copper and tin. One such sea-route, in reverse, was sailed from Cornwall down the French Atlantic coastline as far as the River Garonne where lies today's City of Bordeaux.

According to the map an overland route was then taken, along the Garonne which leads to general south in the direction of the Aude territory, with it's numerous natural springs of both hot and cold water, it's Mediterranean warmth, it's rivers and fair abundance of gold to be mined by Greeks who were more than conversant with the extraction of metal ores. Whilst, no great distance to the east lay the Greek colony of Massalia, Marseille as we know it.

What secrets, I wonder, lie concealed in a land steeped with history, frequently saturated with the shedding of human blood, yet hardly touched in respect of it's unrecorded past?

The Shugborough Monument, Mystery of.

Within the pages of The Holy Blood and The Holy Grail, by Henry Lincoln and co-authors, is a photographic reproduction of the mysterious Shugborough Monument, upon its marble face an engraved image, reversed mirror fashion, of the artist Poussin's celebrated painting with its strange *Et In Arcadia Ego* text.

Underneath the sculptor, upon its plinth, are engraved capital letters in the form of

O.U.O.S.V.A.V.V.

D. . M.

It has long been an unsolved mystery presented by those enigmatic letters.

O·U·O·S·V·A·V·V

D· M·

Nevertheless. I offer my solution.

Why is the bas-relief purposely depicted mirror-fashion? The fact that it is must provide a key to any understanding of what message was concealed within the whole, went my reasoning.

So I listened to my inner voice and reversed the letters to produce

M.V.VA.V.S.O.U.O.D.

Roman numerals MD equate with our 1500. In similar fashion a single V equals 5, three such V's give 15. There are two non-Roman zeroes.

Rarely does one come across the obvious when endeavouring to decypher obscured information from the distant past.

With one of my occasional sideways slips of the mind I decided to place the trio of V's in front of the two zeroes, or 15 followed by the two zeroes to give a numerical value of 1500. I then employed this figure to cancel out the MD 1500.

As a result of this I had a residue of three letters, those of A, S and U. They meant nothing to me.

A second search, of the reversed image, revealed a shepherd's digit pointing between the letters R and C of the word ARCADIA; much of the remainder of lesser definition or too dark to read.

I included both the R and the C with the A, S and U: R.C.A.S.U.

There was something familiar to me, contained within those letters. ARCUS? URCAS? Might they hint at a BEAR?

Forget the C! Artemis! Eureka! Shades of Kallisto! URSA was far-more rewarding. It is non-other than the GREAT BEAR.

Taken in a different context, that of another mystery which belongs with other of my researches, not included here, the BEAR becomes extremely apt.

Members of the wartime Enigma decoding-team were invited to Shugborough Hall with the idea that they investigate the monument with a purpose of seeking a connection with the Holy Grail.

I wrote and proffered my solution in order that they waste no time with searching for a Grail that was never Holy in original concept. No-one had the courtesy to even thank me for my letter. Perhaps someone considered themselves to be far too expert in such a matter, compared with my humble self. However, although that team failed to make progress along intended lines, someone there appears to have been alerted to the possibility that I presented: they made use of that 1500, (with no acknowledgement) in an attempt to present a biblical connection that clearly was a failure.

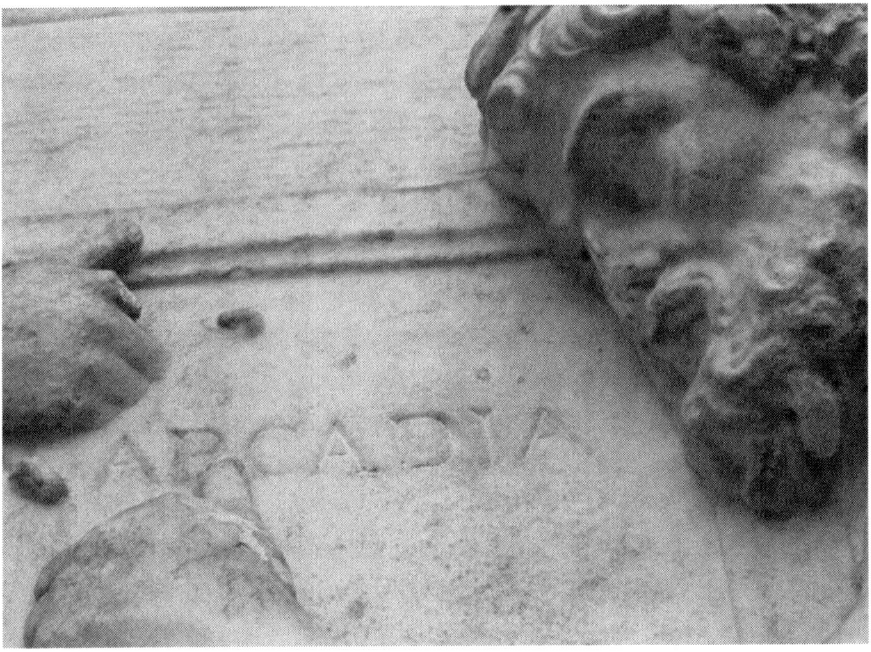

The Lady Godiva.

Provided with a different dressing Lady Godiva can be a more interesting character than legend makes of her, Strip her naked of the image that enshrouds her and bare truth might come to the surface. I am not alone in believing that the story of Godiva is rooted in a pagan past. Study the literature that was composed in an attempt to glorify the woman, seeking out concealed knowledge, and a different picture is revealed. Here, I must admit, that no solid support, to my ideas, is available so far as I am aware. But neither does anything exist to bolster up that which early scribes attach to the lady.

I ask, is it possible that Godiva could have had the bare-faced cheek- all four of them, plus some other rounded parts of her anatomy- to strip herself naked and create the first recorded instance of a female streaker in public view? And could she have put on that bold front amidst multi-storeyed buildings of Elizabethan construction, bordering cobbled streets leading to Coventry's market place? I think not for a variety of reasons.

Firstly: Around 1000 AD Coventry held no known charter which gave its people the right to hold a weekly market.

Secondly: At that time Coventry was little more than a small village, a hamlet of wattle and daub dwellings surrounded by a part of the Forest of Arden where dwelt its labour-force in conical huts such as charcoal-burners might erect.

Thirdly: The population of greater Coventry, at that time, is estimated to be no more than 1200 persons of whom many were scattered about the village and its forested environs. Other locals would include those higher up the social scale, ecclesiastic persons whose church of wood must have been somewhat draughty.

Fourthly: There exists no record which shows Godiva to have held any permanent home at Coventry. She may never have placed trim-shod feet anywhere in the place. One source says that she was very friendly towards the Abbot of Evesham, while suggesting that she might have been buried close alongside her friend.

Fifthly: Coventry, of nine to ten centuries ago, had no cobbled thoroughfare let alone Elizabethan houses. And, therefore, no buildings with shuttered windows for any Peeping Tom from which to look out. It's tracks would have been of beaten earth, mud up to the knee-caps in foul weather.

Sixthly: Unlike the reason behind Godiva's escapist ride, that of freeing the people from excessive taxation, it was slavery that she hoped to eradicate. It is highly unlikely that Leofric could have responded, had he wished to do so in his own right, when obeying his wife's attempt at blackmail, since his king, under the Church's guiding-hand, was final arbiter in matters of that importance.

There is one further point that I find to be out of character with the lady's time; how could a Church, forever condemning Eve, when Adam was the weaker party, endeavour to treat so piously our second naked lady?

Nonetheless, legends of this type, as with true myth, are likely to hide something of factual interest. .

Some two centuries, following the demise of Lady Godiva, a church cleric, named Roger of Wendover, penned the original legend relating to her. It was he who first informed us of that delightful morsel of naked equestrianism. It was he who wrote her name, spelt Godagifu, not Godiva as we know of it.

Godagifu is a pious renderring of Goda Geofu, Godagifu being interpreted as Gift of God, with Goda Geofu meaning Gift of Goda.

Goda Geofu was a goddess of Germanic origins, according to one source. Robert Graves places Goda as being Celtic. I see no reason to quibble over this. The first Celts originated in an area of the Europe which we know as Germany.

There is a Runic symbol in the form of an X, or Greek Cross with equal arms. Runic X denotes a gift. Gifts are presented at Xmas. Lovers make gifts of kisses at the foot of love-letters, as well as SWALK. The birth of a healthy child, or a fine harvest of crops, would be accepted as a Gift of Goda. Goda, as goddess, can be directly associated with Venus, Greek Aphrodite. Goda was also Queen of the Mayday rite of fertility, the springtime rite of Ancient Greece in which a variety of goddesses were represented, including Artemis.

Tradition has it that Goda adopted a certain formula when presiding over the aforementioned rite. She stripped herself naked, covered her nudity with a net and climbed upon the back of a goat which would carry her to her venue. She would have been accompanied by a hare, symbolic of The Chase, while conversing with oracular raven/crow. Some say that she held an onion between her teeth, but this would be unlikely for it appears to be unique to folklore in general. An apple would be far more in keeping with the ritual, a sacred apple which is to be found connected with rites of fertility and sacrificial kings. Below I will reveal such an apple in a myth that bares a close parallel with that of Goda's legendary rite.

At the site of Coventry's cathedral ruins there lies a large piece of rough stone upon which are inscribed the figures of a naked female who is covered by a net, a hare, a crow, most likely a raven and an apple. These are all elements linked with sacrifice of a sacred king, dating at least back to an era preceding Homer's Greece by centuries. From such early sources we can trace that which Goda had afoot.

Goda would set her goat-mount on the move, her hare already released to show her in which direction to travel. Boudicea, too, possessed a magical hare, an ancient character in folklore which signifies The Chase, as it did for the Queen of the Iceni who directed her Celtic warriors to follow the animal and to attack legions of foreign invaders.

Some Greek goddesses had nets with which to capture their sacred king-consorts prior to their eventual sacrifice.

Once she had netted her victim Goda would present him with her golden apple, his unfailing passport to some glorious Valhalla, Elysian-fields, Avalon or other Garden of Eden. Goda, doubtless knowledgeable in the lores of Nature, would have made preparations for her hare to follow a certain path, whilst she alone could interpret her raven's chatter.

In Greek mythology there exist many variations on the ritual sacrifice of the sacred-king, under matriarchal rule when deities of the female aspect far outnumbered male equivalents, and were, naturally, the superior sex.

In order to gain favour for the tribe's good health, abundant offspring, and profusion of crops, supplications to the Great Mother consisted primarily in the sacrifice of a virile male previously prepared for the task, his after-death destination assured. We call it Heaven. But his would be more rewarding than that; wine, women and song, perhaps until the end of time. Such sacrifices were formally a twice-annual event, taking place at the winter or summer solstices, major divisions of the solar year that personified both death and re-birth in a natural cycle.

Natural cycles in Nature were of far greater importance to our early forebears than they are to us with our almanacs, clocks and television to remind us of the passage of time, and possibly of what the future holds for us, assuming that the politician's verbal entrails have been correctly decyphered.

Drugged, most likely with an ambrosia of barley-porridge, honey, and wine, with a further constituent of Aminata Muscaria- the magic mushroom- the victim would be so full of bliss that he would be prepared to take on all of the Tritons single-handed in a test of strength. There exist many people of today, who are ready to face death for the sake of religious beliefs and heavenly rewards.

Goda's victim would obligingly copulate with her or, rather, her female, priestess-representative. What healthy male could refuse a goddess her demands of copulation? In this context, it was an act containing a sacred element allied to fertility which same would be enhanced when the man's blood was ceremoniously sprinkled upon the ground with future benefit to crops, and all that consumed them, in mind.

When Goda set out upon her goat, she trailed one foot in a water-filled ditch, apple between her teeth, her nakedness covered by a net. That is to say that Goda was neither on land nor upon water, neither fasting nor feasting, neither dressed nor undressed.

There stands a very close parallel with the above, which relates to Agamemnon. Agamemnon-*Very Resolute*-is described as having a net thrown over his head whilst standing naked, one foot in water inside the palace annex, the other upon it's marble slabs. Which is to say that he was neither on land nor in water, neither inside the palace nor outside of the palace, neither dressed nor undressed. To complete the analogy a goddess-figure places an apple between Agamemnon's teeth. He was, therefore, neither fasting nor feasting. He was, nonetheless, to be sacrificed, as the apple denotes.

Godiva is assumed to have ridden upon a white horse. The colour, here, has nothing in common with virginity; it is lunar. And horses were venerated by the Goddess, if white in colour. Goda had her net. Godiva had her locks to hide her nudity. Since she had no market-place to which to ride, just where was she aiming? When Peeping Tom was later introduced to the tale, had someone in mind the myth of Artemis and Actaeon?

Christmas-day seems to be an example of religious tampering with former Old Religion conviviality. The Church of Rome was increasingly aware that the older Yuletide, twelve days of celebration, was deeply heretical in that it's revellers payed far more attention to it than they did to Christmas Day itself. As Yule commenced with the winter solstice, when the old Year ends and the New is born, those revellers had a few days in which to become so deeply engrossed with it, whilst being far too full of the wrong type of spirit, that the Christian festival was arriving and leaving without their noticing it. Short of putting the fear of God into them by threatening wholesale excommunication, there was only one thing to do. And the Pope did it.

Yuletide is essentially a celebration of the New Year: 'We will move the date of that solar-orientated New Year. We will ignore the sun and place the New Year after our own sacred day. And that is how our year became eleven days slow in relation to sun-time. Game, set and match to Gregory of papal fame!

I wondered what date, if any, Roger of Wendover had in mind when he wrote the myth of Godiva? How was it that a woman, who volunteered to ride naked of body upon the back of a horse, should receive so much acclaim from men of her church, a church that continued to decry naked Eve, and to see all women being inferior to men? Surely Adam could have shown more self-control! So do not cast stones!

That Genesis piece of biblical mythology is intended to indicate that female deities, once superior, were now subservient to a recently-invented exclusive god, a single, male counterpart. The same demotion was in progress all around the Middle East, at that time, Woman being *'Put in her place'*.

Cast your mind back to Southam, a well-known centre for practising of witchcraft into more recent days. It's diocese came under the jurisdiction of the Coventry monastery, courtesy of Leofric, Godiva's second husband, Godiva who, according to record, worshipped not the male deity but the Virgin, almost with manic fervour, it appears. Roger of Wendover calls Godiva *'a true worshipper and lover of the Mother of God'* That lady, for reasons known only to herself, gave preference to the female in her creed of religious worship. In spite of the Church's efforts to force everyone to toe the ecclesiastic line it was unable to govern their innermost thoughts. One might easily equate the Mother of God with whomsoever one chose, in the mind which no-one else could read. This is most likely (see below) what the good monk was up to with his Great Mother, goddess figure. Perhaps , in her given name, Godiva (Godagifu) found a stimulating reminder of her name-sake, Goda Geofu.

As to the date when Godiva rode into legend is concerned, stained-glass windows, commemorating the lady and her husband, might hold a clue. It is solely from remnants of the windows, and the written word, that something might be revealed.

In one of those windows Godiva was depicted as holding a white-blossomed bough. This would suggest springtime when buds commence to come into flower, Today white hawthorn blossoms around mid-May, hence it's sobriquet of May-blossom. May-flowers have five petals and are, therefore, goddess-related in colour and number, five being a pentagonal number associated with a pentagram of five equally-spaced apogee-points that the planet Venus reaches during each of it's eightfold years passage throughout the night-skies. The Ancients knew of this. Apple-blossom arrives at about the same time, and has five petals, predominantly white in colour.

Without that eleven days modification to our calendar those flowers would make their appearances at the time of Mayday of Old.

There was a further window of stained-glass in which Godiva is depicted in triplicate, one portrayal larger in size than it's neighbours to either side; a moon at the full accompanied by its lesser crescents?

When searching for a myth's hidden elements it is all too easy to overlook some seemingly insignificant aspect that may hold a meaning of interest. But for a change of mental direction that disguised facet might remain unexplored. Here I make another diversion from legend to something which, although legendary, is more widely known.

To Christians the Serpent of Old has overtones of evil. Perhaps the most famous-or infamous-example of such a creature is that which *'spake with human tongue'*, the serpent which lay within the confines of a biblical Paradise, a Garden of Eden, and another abstraction analogous of all paradises in folklore and myth.

Now take Eve, a lovely little charmer deserving of goddess status, as her name implies.

The name Eve is firmly-rooted in Hebrew Hiwa, in turn, directly derived from Hawwa/Hewwa Pronounce Ws as Vs. Hewwa is to be seen as Mother of All Living, an important Hittite goddess. In non-Christian paradises it was the Wise Serpent that guarded the Gates, a true representative of life - eternal for reason which follows.

Snakes annually slough their skins. To the Ancients this would have appeared to be miraculous, they not being of the David Attenborough ilk. Any living form, that is capable of perambulation would normally die if it lost it's skin. But snakes did not die; they came *'back to life'*.

They were regenerated and thereby took on sacred proportions. Such Magic!

Although Eve's apple appears to be a late insertion it remains meaningful in that Greek goddesses, or their counterparts on Earth, their priestesses, bestowed sacred apples upon divine kings who were to be ritually sacrificed, heroes one and all like Agamemnon, Achilles, Heracles and company.

When morally-defunct Adam capitulated to Eve's overwhelming beauty, and copulated with her, that lady's golden apple should have indicated the end of him with his one-way ticket to the Land of Eternal Youth.

The heads of some heroes were buried at the approaches to a city. Celtic Bran's supposedly guards the approaches to London as Adam's similarly guards the gate to Jerusalem.

So the Lady Godiva bestowed precious gifts upon the inhabitants of a Lincolnshire monastery, gifts of gold in the shape of her bracelets, bracelets worked into the forms of *Serpents*.

I am not done with Coventry, for a lesser myth has arisen in connection with that city. Incidentally, I wonder, when she presented her serpentine gifts, was Godiva's smile as enigmatic as that of Leonardo's Mona Lisa - Lisa of the Moon?

According to expert analysis, by etymologists, researchers into the origins of place-names, the Rivers Severn, Avon, Laughern Brook, and a river in Wales of that latter name, all are of Celtic extraction, each of them sharing an original suffix of-Ferne. Thus we might have Saeferne, Ae-ferne and Lau-ferne.

Beneath the concrete and tarmac of modern Coventry lie two lost rivers, the Couen, also spelt Coven, and the Sherbourne, which met at that point, made their confluence.

For reasons of failing eye-sight, and scribes' terrible handwriting, U's and V's became interchangeable some centuries ago. In like fashion the same can be said of other alphabetic symbols. If Sae-ferne could develop into Severn why not Couen/Coven resulting from Cou-ferne? Anyone who doubts the possibility of such a transition should take up a volume on Place-name Etymology. Much more astonishing are some of the changes!

Late, during the 19th century, deep excavations took place at the Coventry district of Coundon. That work resulted in the discovery of ancient timbers which were later confirmed as formerly providing a river crossing as might exist at a ford, the most sensible place at which to place them where no bridge is available. If ever the Lady Godiva rode upon horseback, in that vicinity, such a ford would have been very convenient.

That there was an early Celtic presence at Coundon is not under dispute. I ask, is it merely coincedental that the Celtic goddess of water-sources went by the appellation of Coventina?

There is a word, both Gallic and Celtic in origin; it is Coun meaning a confluence of rivers. According to Herodotus there existed Celts on the Iberian peninsular who were called by the name of Cunesios. A Professor Ekwell pronounces that Cunetio is Old British-as opposed to Old English. He also tells us that Old Welsh Cune means High, which in turn he translates as Exhalted, Holy.

The second element in Coundon is OE, and applies to a hill. This is an example of a marriage of two tongues, Coun being Celtic.

We now have Coun, Couen, Cunesios, Cunetio, Cune and Coven, all with the same basic root. We have it in the various steps that produced the eventual Coventry, of which the earliest-known form is Couantree. Cofentreo appears around 1050 AD, during Godiva's lifetime. It comes close to my suggestion of Co-ferne. A further transformation is Couentre. And there exists a reference to a ford over the River Cune, dated 1355 AD, in a boundary-agreement at Cunetford.

Cunetford establishes the fact that there was once a ford in the vicinity of the confluence between the Rivers Couen and Sherbourne. If we accept Professor Ekwells Exhalted in relation to Cune, Couen and et cetera, then we have a double blessing in that OE Sherbourne has the meaning of Bright Water. Sher is that same as is to be seen in the female name of Shirley, meaning something in the order of Bright Meadow. I have yet to find reference to Goda in association with water. But she did trail one foot in that liquid.

Etymological experts could find nothing that would confirm the root in the name Coventry. I hope that they will excuse my postulation.

Because of that lack of evidence they produced an hypothesis that Coventry stems from a non-existent Saxon by the name of Coffa, who had a Tree of some note, in the vicinity.

When one considers that Coventry was once engulfed inside the Forest of Arden I doubt if Old Coffa could see his tree for woods. So Coffa, plus his Tree are the elements upon which the hypothesis is founded.

A second hypothesis. My hypothesis!

First I will inform you that the Coffa-tree theory is today taken as fact by some people, a modern myth, no less. It was then that I came across the Celtic word, Tre, at a time when I was not engaged in anything remotely connected with Coventry. Celtic Tre means a river fording-place. It becomes obvious, even to a pleiabian such as I: Couen/Coven-Tre. Or, Coven-tre. Or, Coventry.

Peeping Tom

Firstly, when seeking revelation, in the form that it should take, beware of later editions modified to suit prevailing desires. Ovid, male of gender, believer in a patriarchalist system in society where all things female were inferior to their opposite and male equivalent, took up his pen in order to castigate Goddess Artemis, giving her the role of villainess whilst elevating Actaeon to the realm of Heroes. This is a deliberate modification of original myth, slanted to suit male egoes..

According to Ovid, Actaeon, great huntsman, was turned into a Stag by Artemis who set his own hounds upon him to tear him to pieces, because he boasted of being her superior in the art of hunting. What a hypocrite was Ovid.

Artemis stands naked, bathing herself at a magical font in an annual renewal of her virginity. Along comes dastardly Actaeon who sees the goddess and ogles her gorgeous nudity. Artemis takes note of this intrusion into that rite which no man should observe, the penalty for so doing being death to the culprit.

Artemis, quite reasonably, turns Actaeon into a Stag and hunts him down with her own pack of hounds. She is, after all, a goddess. I explore this myth at greater length, later.

In addition to my examination of the Godiva legend; I am satisfied that the Goda/Mayday rite of fertility lurks underneath the surface of Roger of Wendover's story of the lady. As to the Horned God associated with the rite, particularly among mediaeval witches, he is Pan who seduced Selene as Maiden and Virgin aspect of the Lunar Goddess triad This is a reflection of May-eve orgies when the Queen of the May rode upon the Upright Man's back to celebrate their Greenwood marriage, the ritual much modified since the time preceding Homer. Pan was formerly seen in the guise of a horned goat, later becoming a Ram. They ain't 'arf mucked about with the early version, even our Queen of the May a virgin only by the good offices of a selection-committee that ignores rumour and hearsay, as often as not. They have a most difficult task to perform. And those maypole ribands should be coloured white, red and black to denote the May-queen's transition from Virgin to Nymph to Old Crone.

Peeping Tom for the role of Actaeon!

The Monk's Poem.

Whatever a person's religious beliefs, or lack of, I think that they will readily acknowledge the beauty of the following poem. It is a translation from the Latin, and provides evidence of the existence of goddess-worship about one century after the death of Godiva. The monk wrote these words during twelfth-century England, a ceremonial incantation for the correct gathering of medicinal herbs.

Holy Goddess Earth, Parent of Nature, who dost generate all things and regenerate the Planet which Thou showest to folk on Earth, Thou, Guardian of the Heavens, and seas, and arbiter of all the gods, by whose influence Nature is wrapt in silence and slumber.

Thou art She who restoreth day and putteth the darkness to flight; Thou who governeth the shades of night in all security, restraining at Thy will the mighty Chaos, winds, rain and storms, or letting them loose. Thou churnest the deep to foam and putteth the sun to flight, and arouseth the tempest or, again, at Thy pleasure, Thou sendeth forth the glad daylight. Thou givest us food in safety by a perpetual covenant and, when our souls fleeth away, it is in Thy bosom that we find our haven of rest. Thou art called, too, by the loving kindness of the gods, The Great Mother who hast conquered the god *of mighty name.*

Thou art the force of Nations and the Mother of the gods, without whom nothing can be born or come to maturity. Mighty art Thou, Queen of the gods! Thou, 0 Goddess, I adore in Thy godhead, and on Thy name I call. Vouchsafe now to fulfil my prayer, and I will give Thee thanks, 0 Goddess, with the faith that Thou deserve. Hear, I beseech Thee, and favour my prayers; vouchsafe to me, 0 Goddess, that for which I pray Thee; grant freely to all Nations upon Earth all herbs that Thy magesty bringeth to life and suffer me thus to gather Thy medicines.

Come to me with healing powers; grant a favourable issue to whatsoever I shall make from these herbs, and may those thrive to whom I administer the same. Prosper, Thou, all Thy gifts to us, for to Thee all things return. Let men take these herbs rightly at my hand. I beseech Thee now, 0 Goddess, may Thy gifts make them whole. Suppliant I beseech Thee that Thy magesty may vouchsafe me this boon.

It is possible that the monk, a member of the Orthodox Church, had two strings to his bow of spiritual persuasions. I, personally, consider him to have been giving strong preference to the Goddess to whom he so ardently prays. After all, it is from the female that all things are born in Nature.

The Vishnu Epic.

Indian mythology tells of Vishnu, a god sleeping among the coils of the Naga Serpent, Ananda. Would this be The Cosmic Serpent of old tradition? In association with this is Brahma, who lives hundred years, each of which is far longer than our Earth-years. Each day Brahma opens and closes his eyes one thousand times. At each opening of the eyes a new world is born. At each closing a world dies. This is mindful of death and re-birth cycles.

Brahma's behaviour is linked to cycles of time, each cycle sub-divided into four divisions, each division called a Yuga.

Krita Yuga represents 1,728,000 Earth-years.
Theta Yuga is of 1,296,000 years.
Dvapara Yuga of 864,000 years.
Kali Yuga of 432,000 years.
I now place those figures in a single column:
1,728,000
1,296,000
864,000
432,000

I decided that they must have an accord with the Sumerian King-lists calculations. But first of all, as with the king-lists, divide the major figure by the lesser; $1,728,000 \div 432,000 = 4$. In fact all three of the greater values are divisible by 432,000, the answers, in descending order, being 4, 3, 2, and 1, of course. Therefore any sub-division of 432,000 must apply to the larger figures.

Common to both king-lists and Stonehenge calculations are the divisors, 30, 19, 360 and 800, the latter being equivalent of 43 x 18.604651. Any lengthy duration of time, which is precisely divisible by 800, must reflect a marriage of lunar-time with that of solar.

That 19 sub-divisor, from the king-lists and Stonehenge, does not apply here, but the 30 can be applied, as can other divisors of 360.

$$432,000 \div 30 = 14400$$
$$14,400 \div 360 = 40.$$
$$432,000 \div 18.604651 = 23,220.$$
$$23,220 \div 43 = 540 \ (30 \times 18).$$
$$432,000 \div 800 = 540.$$

Any such enormous lengths of time, contained within the mythology of the Ancients, no matter which land of origin, when precisely divisible by 800, must represent a strict coincidence of lunar-cycles measured against solar-cycles, these latter being Sidereal.

I have shown how this was achieved at Stonehenge. The question therefore arises, did the Sumerians possess a physical observatory by which to make possible their king-lists recordings? Does something of that order, remain with us, awaiting recognition of what purpose it once served?

During recent years we were treated to a televised programme relating to the Temple of Ankara, also spelt Angora. Here, again, the figure 1,728,000 popped up from among the temple layout. And again some extravagant theories.

And now, whilst maintaining the lunar theme, but on a lighter note, to The Round Table.

One Round Table of Renown.

My work with the Sumerian King-lists caused me to take a closer look at Layamon's account of the building of the Round Table on behalf of a fellow by the name of Arthur. On that occasion I read with extra attention to detail. Those details I took step by step, each one isolated from the remaining text. In that manner perhaps some feint gleam of light might be seen, shining from beneath a gloss of colourful garlanding. The following are the elements that I selected for further investigation.

A Cornish tree-worker volunteered to build a round table.

More than 1600 knights were fighting for supremacy, their ranks being a disorderly lot.

Four weeks were required for the table's construction.

I asked myself why Layamon used the term *tree-worker* rather than carpenter? Why should the man be Cornish? Why that particular county? It was later that I saw a possible connection. There are Standing Stones, and the like, in Cornwall. That area is as Celtic as is Wales.

What could knights fighting for precedence imply other than that which was on the surface? Permissible or not I began to think in terms of *nights*.

More than 1600 knights/nights. Why not state the actual figure? Or did Layamon purposely employ 1600 in order to bring attention to that figure?

And, rather than accept the more obvious, just what were the knights truly fighting over?

That period of four weeks, during which the tree-worker would construct his circular table, is fairly precise. It is not four months, four years, nor is it a little over nor under that amount of time. But four weeks is that which we generally speak of as one month lunar, a common generalization. Moon would be derived from OE Mona of the same meaning.

Prior to making a more-searching study of the above I placed our Round Table under greater scrutiny.

Assuming that each fully-armoured knight would be in need of two feet-linear as a minimum of breathing space, when seated at the table, a large circumference would be required for so dainty a piece of furniture. Its circumference would be

$$1600 \times 2\text{-feet} = 3200 \text{ feet,}$$

or close on 1067 yards. From that figure we achieve a diameter of $1067 \div pi = 339.636$ yds. which can be rounded off to 340 yds. This, in turn, gives a radius of $340 \div 2 = 170$yds.

$$170 \times 170 = 90792.0 \text{square yards.}$$

There are 4840 square yards in one acre.

$$90800 \div 4840 = 18.76 \text{ acres.}$$

By comparison the area of a standard football pitch encompasses $100 \times 120 = 12000$square yards.

$$12,000 \div 4840 = 2.479 \text{acres.}$$

Therefore such a Round Table would possess an area equivalent of $18.76 \div 2.479 = 7.567$, little more than 7.5 football pitches of area.

I would not attempt to guess the weight of such a table, nor how many prime oaks would require felling to merely make it's top let alone it's supports. What weight of nails, coach bolts and screws would be needed? The number of horses that would have been slaughtered to provide sufficient horse-hoof-glue would have left the knights without mounts.

And there is another myth, coming from the film-studios of Hollywood film-studios: those knights of old could never have been as nimble as those portrayed by Hollywood. Their swords alone would weigh thirty pounds or more, avoirdupois. With shields and armour combined with that, only carthorses could have supported them whilst, once hacked to the ground, no knight would have been in a position to jump lightly to his feet, so great was his extra burden.

When I read of that four-weeks period of Layamon's it's lunar links brought an automatic reaction. Could the story, as a whole, hinge around something related to the moon?

Moon implied nights, the reason for my having selected to stop thinking in terms of knights.

I was left with knights fighting for precedence. For me that meant only one thing, and that thing was required to make my hypothesis sound.

Incidentally, Layamon claimed that so huge a table was transportable, could be carried around. What a hope!

Nights and days that accompany one another in changeless order. What else could be meant by the word round? A circle is round. A cycle is often applied to lengths of time. A cycle is round. But I was confronted by a Round Table.

So that is what it is all about; the idea had a nice fit. A calendar is a *table*. A calendar reflects a *cycle* of time measured in days to form a year. Was I able to find a means whereby to introduce that 1600 into my theory? You will recall those amazing king-lists. They held the key.

$$1600 \div 18.604651 = 86: 86 \text{ equals } 43 \times 2.$$

I was not finished.

I returned to Layamon's tree-worker, his carpenter who suggested that a Round Table would solve the problem of many knights causing a mayhem of confusion while battling to decide which one of these should take precedence over all others. Never take any word at its face value when dealing with old myth and legend.

A round table would make them all of equal status with no figurehead seated in the place of honour, as would be the practice with a square or rectangular table. And it was a tree-worker who knew all about construction of round tables. He was, needlessly to say, Cornish.

As I have demonstrated, the figure 19 plays an important role in the mathematics of Stonehenge circles and the Sumerian King-lists. In Cornwall lie the Merry Maidens, a pre-historic circle of 19 stones.

In Cornwall rests a second circle of stones. It is called Boscawen-Un, and contains 19 such stones. Since mention of trees to priestly hierarchies among Celts anywhere in Europe, would bring an automatic association with letters of a tree-alphabet, such as the Beth Luis Nion or Boibel Loth tree-calendar, the former being lunar, it's companion, solar, one might now think in terms of a magical tree-worker. Furthermore, I have presented a lunar aspect in my interpretation of the Round Table story, which now makes Layamon's tree-worker appear to be a man aptly suited to solving the knights problems.

Back to that figure 19, in years the length of reigns for later Greek heroes-cum-sacred kings, a period equivalent 235 lunations. Could our tree-worker have been aware of this? I contend that this is being implied by Layamon. That carpenter, in his home county, had two circles of 19 stones whereby to make calculations by observation.

One solar year contains 12.368746 lunations. 19 times that figure equals 235. 00617, which slight error would be to the sacrificial king's advantage.

$235.0 \div 12.368746 = 18.999501$ years. That king, therefore, would gain for himself a further 5 days on Earth.

There may be those who would disagree with my proposition that the Round Table was in fact a lunar calendar. They are free to so do. But, in the above I made use of the numbers, 19, 43 and 18.6. The very same as some from my king-lists mathematics and from Stonehenge. Was Arthur's legendary Grail to be found at Stonehenge by those who had the secret knowledge in those numbers?

The previous Beth Luis Nion calendar was composed of thirteen months, 13 x 28, plus one day per annum. They now had the Boibel Loth calendar of twelve months, 12 x 30, plus five floating days per annum. And under the tutelage of Sun-god Apollo. Trouble had hit in their priestly heads. How did one deal with five floating days per year? But it was worse than that. There was that 0.25636 of a day that would cause mayhem with the passage of time, too. Stonehenge calculators were not involved with that, they being lunar inclined and made adjustable to another time-scale. There was much scratching of ignoble heads at the Court of King Arthur. But they were far too proud to acknowledge Woman's superiority in learned matters, too proud to ask them to unveil their secret key by which to unlock the older calendar's mysteries. And thus was mounted a hunt for the Grail.

Lancelot, somewhere along the route, when off a-questing, met up with three rather strange females, a trio or triad of ladies. His objective was the temple at Stonehenge where solar and lunar time, he hoped, could be brought together with great accuracy if one knew the Secret of the Circles. It was there that Apollo made his appearances every 19 years; as near as makes no difference, 235 lunations, assuming that one was an initiate, and no problem unless one sought even greater accuracy required in the sending of satellites to orbit Jupiter and places beyond.

By one means or another, basic mathematical values, to be found at Stonehenge, would provide a solution whereby priests to Apollo/Arthur could place their knights/nights back in order of merit. They should have lain off the mead when junketing at their Round Table.

Robert Graves created the word, Iconography, meaning, in general, the practice of deliberate alteration to original myth, especially to promote patriarchalism above that of matriarchalism, of gods over goddesses, of Man over Woman.

In his personal re-writing of the Artemis/Actaeon legend Ovid, in causing Artemis to be the villainess of the story, he is merely making use of Graves' iconography, a technique adopted by male historians of past and present. Compared with mortal Taleisin Bill Shakespeare was only an aspiring bard. At down to earth, fundamental levels, Henry, the fifth to bear the name, was no hero. He was more a blood-lusting bandit who pillaged, whored and looted with great zest. I, for one, sympathize with no-nonsense Artemis, and I would treat, with equal contempt, any Peeping Tom!

The Merry Maidens.

The title of this circle of 19 stones in Cornwall, is derived, according to legend, from impious young girls turned to stone because of their habit of dancing at that spot in defiance of the Sabbath law against such joyful activities.

An older name, for those stones, is Dans Maen, corrupted to Dawn's Men when, in fact, translation of Dans Maen gives Stone Dance. As I reveal, elsewhere, Merry has a variety of connotations with the pre-Christian Mary.

Here, then, are two more examples of Greek Meton's equivalent of the lunar-associated 19 figure from both Sumerian King-lists and Stonehenge calculations.

Arthur of Legend.

Arthur, lecherous as any stone-faced gargoyle, a man who will commit incest at the rip of a maidenly veil, a man of free-wheeling habit whose parentage is rather suspect, in the moral sense, a man lascivious to the hilt of his phallic Excalibre, becomes a hero, all debauchery overlooked. Sounds like some Greek hero, an Ajax accused of performing the despicable act of necrogenic lust after falling in love with the still-warm corpse of an Amazon queen whom he had just slain.

Arthur should never have become a man to admire, that unscrupulous bigot. But knight-of-old, be they ever so bold, did assume the right to deflower any beauteous maiden who was unfortunate enough to be caught in an unguarded moment with a garter in view. And in full armour?

He was one of' a chivalrous company, was Perceval-Pierce the Veil? And Lance-lot took his share of the spoils.

Let poets write of chivalry, they with no hot blood in their veins. Throughout Arthurian romances a-rapin' and a-whorin' is a common occurrence. Had those knights no pride?

Names, both female and male, that appear in Greek mythology, have meanings applicable to status-symbols. In some English surnames the same is to be found. Thatcher; there's a good 'un. During former days Thatcher would apply to someone who thatched buildings. One has to start somewhere! Carpenter, Tyler, Farmer, and so on, came from trades pursued.

Some persons are unfortunate in choice of diminutive. To Greeks of Old, Cilla meant She-ass. Think on it Arne! Pronounced in like fashion with Arnie, inferred Ewe-lamb. I do not invent these.

As to Scylla, I will not take chances with that one. For Thetis read Disposer: Typhon. Smoke that Stupefies or, High Wind. And Ariadne was Most Pure.

How many New Yorkers are mighty proud of their city's designation of Big Apple whilst unaware that there exists a cabbage with the same appellation? Now to Artemis.

Artemis, Of the Net, Of the Three Ways, Whitish but not Dark, which latter probably refers to her lunar, maiden aspect, a slender waxing crescent portion of the moon with the remainder in darkness, sometimes vaguely visible. Of the Net-which could also apply to a few other of her sister-goddesses,-would be a reference to the net used in the capture of a future scared king who would be ritually sacrificed for the good of the tribe.

Arthurianologists take note: Artemis was also Lady of the Lake for she has an indirect link with Arthur.

One female character, mentioned in things Arthurian, is Britomart whom the First Earl of Warwick, and Knight of the Round Table, Artegall, married. The Warwicks' coat of arms depicts an upright Bear. Artemis, too, was known as The Upright, her totem animal The Bear in her homeland of Arcadia.

In his Faerie Queene Spencer introduces Britomart. She is his Warrior Maiden, mindful of Artemis, The Huntress, with crescent bow and pack of hounds.

Britomart is based upon Cretan Britomartis, suddenly made true Brit, in the minds of some. Britomartis has all the characteristics of Artemis for her name is yet another sobriquet for Artemis. We find Britomartis Dictynna-*Of the Net*,- as we also find Artemis Dictynna. Artemis originated in Crete, as did her brother Apollo, male and, therefore her inferior. In Minoan Crete the Goddess ruled supreme. Artemis was Virgin Maiden. Britomartis means Bright Maiden!

Artegall, First Earl of Warwick, et cetera, married Britomart, whose roots are in Crete and Artemis, is said to have borne the arms of Achilles, Achilles a Greek hero, and sacrificial king. That laming, in the hero's heel with a poisoned arrow, is significant in that such a laming, be it elsewhere on the body, infers that the victim is shortly to be sacrificed to his goddess by whatever name she bears.. Laming also came to mean emasculating.

Artegall now provides yet another Greek connection through the military arms of Achilles. He must have been a foolhardy fellow to marry a Britomart/Artemis, for any human to take such a step was destined to be sacrificed to her.

With Artemis, through Britomart/Britomartis, in the Arthurian saga, Apollo, her twin must be somewhere nearby.

He is! He is to be found in Pelias who was succeeded by his son , Lucius who, in turn, was succeeded by Apollo who unwittingly married his own mother. Not surprising with Old Arthur setting questionable examples.

In matriarchal Greece a king's marriage to his mother implied that he was acting as consort for a specific number of months or years, prior to his being sacrificed to the Goddess. He was, in fact, married to the Goddess.

Apollo means Apple-man. And apples played an important role in sacred-king sacrifices.

Take note of the prefix element in the name Artegall, that of Art. There is also the Warwicks' heraldic Bear to keep in mind.

It is said that the name Arthur is derived from one of two sources that is Welsh Arth gwyr or Celtic Arto Viros, otherwise Bear Man. Incidentally, Artegall would have felt at home in the Forest of Arden.

The name Arden is rooted directly in Ardennes, of the Franco-Belge forest and vicinity. And there were bears in the Forest of Arden, in the past.

Well into our era, at least the early fourteenth century, Cults of the Bear prevailed in the Ardennes Forest, papal forces finally ordered to expunge that heresy.

The goddess, worshipped by those Bear-cults, was known as Arduina, which is a version of Artemis to whom people paid homage in Arcadian Greece, and whose totem animal was the Bear.

Art and Ard are very much alike in pronunciation. They occur in Arthur, Artegal, Arden, Ardennes, Artemis, Arduina and in the names of two areas bordering the Ardennes forest.

In one French romance Arthur had an uncle by the name of Ardan.

I have made no exhaustive study of Arthurian legend, and there may be other remaining evidence of a Greek influence. Artemis was, of course, the original *Lady of the Lake*. Not only was Artemis the original Lady of the Lake but any would-be consort to a queen who represents such a goddess upon Earth, must prove his worthiness, by his extraction of a sword from a mountain-side cleft in a rock.

Heracles, Theseus, and other Greek heroes had their Twelve Labours to perform, in advance of being sacrificed to the Goddess. Arthur, too, had his Twelve Battles before succumbing to his wounds, following which he was transported to the Isle of Avalon, direct equivalent of the Greek Elysian Fields, both of them orchards of apples.

A careful search of a detailed map of Brittany would reveal two places, the illusive Lyonnais, one of them.. I do not imply that Arthur was of French blood. There is also that mysterious Forest of Broceliande (Now the Forest of Paimpont) in a Brittany formerly as Celtic as Cornwall or Wales. Arthur made at least one appearance in the Broceliande forest.

If anyone should doubt that any Aegean influences reached into Arthurian legend they should note that which is about to follow. Elements from the distant past are with us today, should one take the trouble to examine their origins.

Someone once claimed that there is nothing new under the sun. They may well be correct in that basic, human needs in life remain unaltered. There are those, however, which come in modified form, not necessarily to our liking. Slings and spears, bows and arrows have been replaced by the daemons of modern warfare that do not distinguish between civilian and combatant, no matter what the claims of we-are-holier-than-thou, five-star generals demonstrating highly-edited versions of reality.

Myths come in many guises when civilian doubts are to be placated. It is rare that you will see pictorial evidence of the one that missed. This same factor applies when true myth has been modified, some facet deliberately overlooked, altered to suit prevailing egoes. When male gods gained ascendancy over former goddess, those female deities became downgraded and vilified for reinforcement of priestly designs.

Nevertheless, truth will always surface if one digs deeply enough with the sharp spade of inquisitiveness, So how can a king, of recent date show a trace of goddess-worship?

Kings, representative of Heads of State, must at all times display a fair degree of wisdom, even though that should require the services of professional speech-makers who deliver the usual telling phrase or unaccustomed wit for which the monarch will assume responsibility, thereby enchanting his people. Kings must at all times give an impression of god-like invincibility when under the public gaze, which demands at least a modicum of robust health.

Some four millennia into the past Minoan kings had their cheeks artificially glossed with a few dabs of rouge. This practice was employed by English, and British kings even as late as George, the sixth monarch to bear the name.

No-one will love a sickly king, show him respect, or be prepared to die for him. Kings reflect the state of a nation; therefore a physically impaired monarch would have a psychological effect upon a populace unwilling to do battle on his behalf. Potential enemies would swiftly take advantage of that air of disinclination, for kingships supplied the foundations whereby a nation grew strong or weak.

Consider heraldry, our Prince of Wales Feathers, to be precise. That design is a modification of the French Fleur de Lys, which we known by the name of Iris, emblematic of Gallic kings throughout the centuries.

These are, too, to be seen in any *trinity* of lunar goddesses, be they Selene, Athene, Hecate or any other combination according to time and place. Face rouged, a Minoan king would be noticeable in his badge of office, his purple-iris flower suitably emblazoned, *trinity* of major petals openly displayed. Purple remained the principal colour in regents' official refinery, and continues to do so in these supposedly enlightened times.

The king, perhaps bound with green withy-wands, was destined for the sacrificial altar in order that his people should live free of all want under the all-seeing eye of their particular goddess, one man destroyed for the benefit of all. Napalm is far less discerning in the eye of any deity, one would hope.

White swans were under the protection of the Goddess. Is our present monarch made the more divine as Protectoress of Swans?

Wassailing is one of our older customs, as is the beating of trees to rid them of evil spirits and to facilitate future, heavy crops of fruit. Former Greeks made use of the practice, too.

From Triple Goddess to the Church of Rome which too has it's own triad in it's Holy Trinity.

Mistletoe; according to arboreal authority the British oak does not provide a suitable host-tree for the growth of mistletoe. East European oaks, on the other hand, do. Our apple and poplar would perform the task far more eloquently.

Mistletoe, beneath which Goda's gifts (kisses) are exchanged, is small, white berry of spherical shape, a moon in miniature. Mistletoe was sacred to the Great Athene; Athene the Wise, born out of the head of Zeus, so later mythogrophers would have it. Maybe that is why Thunder-Balls Zeus behaved so madly, having no wisdom to call his own after Athene left his thick head. Mistletoe was Athene's Herb of Regeneration, her Heal-all.

When mistletoe was cut, under matriarchal rule, for purposes of ceremony with the Goddess looking on, it would have been cropped with a miniature sickle constructed, perhaps with slivers of obsidian-glass fixed into a crescent-shaped backing of bone, ivory or wood. The ritual cutting of mistletoe would have heralded the founding of a city, as occurred at Rome with semi-divine twins present, one of whom the sacred king, the other his tanist. The latter would kill the other in a form of sacrifice, then reign in his stead. I read one version of the story of Romulus and Remus, and vague it was in terms of myth. But Romulus does die. He is 'murdered' I discovered. One should at all times be suspicious of divine twins, such as are to be found in the Bible, for instance. In that book are many instances of female deities being-downgraded in favour of the male..

From mistletoe to Guinevere. There are other spellings of the lady's name, but this above suits my objective.

French Gui denotes mistletoe. Arthur's Guinevere is thought of as being dressed in white. With that scurrilous villain around I bet she was no virgin. But white is one of the Triple Goddess colours, that of the Maiden-virgin aspect. Guinevere, to whom Arthur appears to have been married, in some form or other, disappears and reappears upon three separate occasions. Who could blame the lady?

Those three vanishing-acts remind me of the three phases of the moon, waxing, full and waning aspects. We have a Guinevere in triplicate, one might say and, through the Gui element in her name, might well be associated with Athene's Heal-all of regenerative properties, her mistletoe.

Morgan le Fay, allegedly Arthur's half-sister, presided over Avalon, chief among nine sisters. Nine is the number of death in goddess-related mythology, as is three.

Morgan le Fay is said to have lived at the time of the Trojan War. She is also reputed to have a daughter called by the name, Pulzella, Gaia, or Gaea, which is a further name for the Mother-Earth goddess. This makes Morgan a goddess, too. The author of Sir Gawain and the Green Knight refers to Morgan as goddess. Green Knight; Green Man of the May Eve rites, and eventual death of the sacred king?

What then of Elaine, daughter of Pelles who tricked Lancelot into sleeping with the girl thinking that she was Guinevere. The daughter was also known as The White.

The name Elaine is a form of Helen, Helen of Greek mythology, which same name means Moon, or a basket constructed of sacred withy-wands, with which to make offerings to the Moon-goddess. Athene, and other of her sister goddesses, had that White appendage.

Helen of Troy, and all of those heroes, some of them as dastardly as Arthur himself, might well be the character upon whom Morgan le Fay is loosely based, while Ajax, Achilles, and fellow actors, take the roles of sacrificial king. A further element might suggest that an Arthurian connection lies in magical Excalibur.

His withdrawal of a sword from a rocky cleft confirmed Arthur's kingship. This same honour was bestowed upon Early-Greek consorts to a queen-priestess, for they, too, would withdraw a sword from a cleft of rock.

As for Merlin, he is to be associated with the Stag, as was Artemis, the Stag signifying a human soul. In another direction Merlin has an affiliation with the Celtic Stag-horned god, Cernunnos.

Please refrain from laughter: the king, who ruled over Avalon, was called Bangon!

In addition to the foregoing I find that, in accordance with Welsh tradition, Arthur was 'One of the Crimson Ones'. I find this to be suggestive of Minoan kings whose cheeks were rouged in preparation for a rite of sacrifice, albeit of a surrogate.

That Apollo unwittingly marries his mother does not imply an incestuous arrangement. Beneath the surface it indicates his marriage to the Goddess, which is to say, despite of his godlike status, a Hero being sacrificed to her, The Mother Goddess.

So, through Artegall, Britomartis is introduced to the legend. Britomartis is also Cretan Artemis before the latter was installed in Arcadia by invading Greeks. Among her many epithets Artemis is the original Lady of the Lake. Cretan Apollo, male and brother to Artemis, would be his sister's inferior in a matriarchal society. Only much later does he become the Solar-god following upon the enforced demotion of feminine deities in company with a upsurge in patriarchalism.

As you will observe from above, the prefixes ART and ARD, can be traced from north-western Europe back to Arcadia and thence to Artemis whose totem beast is the BEAR, a bear which is to be found in the name of ARTHUR, he who is to be associated with Artemis in her position as LADY of the LAKE.

And, in Ancient Greece, any would-be queen's consort must prove his suitability by first withdrawing a sword from a rocky cleft.

Fenris.

I once dreamt that I observed myself standing upon a barren plain, brown in colour, to my fore beyond this, distant snow-topped mountains.

Suddenly, to my far right something moved at the horizon. It then approached me from the right, moving at terrific speed and hugging the ground. As it passed by me, from right to left, I saw that it had a grey and white head, but more in appearance to a heavy cloud in density. Attached to this head was a tail, miles in length, and the head taking on the features of a wolf, the whole resembling a comet, hence the speed I supposed.

It was two weeks following this that I selected a library book upon Norse legend as a part of my research into legend in general. At that moment I had never knowingly heard of Fenris. Fenris was the name given to a comet from Norse legend, with the head of a *Wolf!*

Upon occasion this type of **coincedence** does occur for me, a useful adjunct to the researcher once in awhile.

You will recall those stupendous lengths of time as portrayed in the mythology of lands elsewhere, of Sumeria, India and Cambodia, and from the records of Chaldean priest/historian Berossus. In each case figures, representative of monumental spans of time, can be reduced to fundamental levels by employment of the same basic, numerical formula. In this is the key-divisor of 18.604651.

One reads of Valhalla, it's gods, it's 500 gates plus 40 more, and of the 800 Heroes, the Einherier thereof, who issue forth from each gate to do battle with Fenris and company of Frost Giants, of Midgard the Fearsome, and Serpent et cetera.

Multiply that 800 by 500 + 40, or 800 x 540, and the answer is 432,000, this last figure floating about in time-spans from Cambodia, the Indian Vishnu Epic, Berossus, and who knows where else from widespread folklore?

And what is more, 432,000 divided by 4 equals 10800, which is the number of bricks in an Indian fire-altar. 1080 is a number favoured, according to John Michell, as a measurement in Indian temple-building from a bygone age.

And with the Precession of the Equinoxes, of 25920 years, favoured by professional readers of future events, rather than stir a stick in the bloody entrails of some poor goat, we can divide 25920 by 1080 to give the figure of 24.

Wherever will it end, my search through figures from the distant past, my bewilderment continuing to grow. However, there is yet one more source wherein large quantities are recorded from, of all places, the Bible.

Solomon's Temple.

To me it seems to be a long time since I discovered the secret contained within the Sumerian King-lists. It appears to be a secret that has wandered across the Northern Hemisphere to be hooked, here and there, by people who wish to maintain a similar numerical secret, a secret that belongs at a time before male deities took supremacy over those of the female gender, lunar goddesses in the ascendancy. It would be a time that is reflected in the religious aspects of early Minoan Crete where Goddess Artemis ranked far higher than her male twin, yet to be elevated above her by Greek invaders of Crete, the High-flying Apollo.

I have been, and continue in like vein, employing a numerical factor of the utmost importance to any understanding of what lay concealed beneath many a huge span of impossible time, time made possible by use of the Lunar Standstill cycle of 18.604651 sidereal years.

One aspect of this playing with numbers surprised me, I must admit. It was that Precession of the Equinoxes connection, brief though it was. Nevertheless, I overlooked one aspect of that which is the Zodiacal division, assuming the modern one of 12.

$$25920 \div 12 = 2160.$$
$$2160 \times 10 = 21600.$$
$$21600 \div 800(18.604651 \times 43) = 27 \text{ easily reduced to } 3.$$
$$432000 \div 2160 = 200 \text{ and et cetera.}$$

These particular numerical connections seem to be the result of Chance.

There is, of course, a famous temple with dimensions of 60 x 30 x 20, that associated with the biblical Solomon, something of a sage, we read. Those dimensions give a volume of 36,000 cubits. It matters not that they are cubits, metres or feet.

This 36,000 is to be found within the Sumerian King-lists as a span of time, one from the ten apparent reigns. But here, in relation to the construction of Solomon's Temple, are other enormous quantities to be given the same numerical treatment. And, too, is a mention of that mysterious 666 of the later book of Revelations.

To more monumental figures contained within the biblical description of the building of a temple for King Solomon, plus its sacred furnishings.

I commence with that temple's dimensions of 60 x 30 x 20 which give a volume of 36000, also to be found in the Sumerian King- lists as the length of one king's reign, therefore subject to the same reduction by use of mathematics of the same principals.

People ask, with the mention of so many talents of gold, where were King Solomon's mines? A simple answer to this question is, with greatly reduced figures, with which to deal, Solomon had no need of such extravagant mines. And this even more so if there never was so grandiose a temple.

First, however, to that Star of David, likewise emblematic of the Seal of Solomon. This six-pointed star originates with Goddess Astarte, by another name biblical Astoreth, she who is one of the Elohim all too briefly referred to in the first Creation myth. Here then my explanation of how Solomon's Temple served for worship of two deities, one female, one male.

When approaching the temple gates one passed between two handsome pillars, Jaichim to one's left, with Boaz to one's right, in word if not in fact.

It is rather ironic that Hebrew Iachem is rooted in Greek Jachem, wealthy Hebrews considering it *au fait* to be well-versed in Greek and one-up over the neighbours. Iachem means *Deadly Hissing Serpent*. And serpents, in association with goddess-figures, were held to possess powerful magic. Can you shed your skin and live after the event? They also guarded the gates to many an Isle of the Blessed, Elysian Fields and such glorious lands of the hereafter. If one accepts the Garden of Paradise at face-value the serpent is also extremely knowledgeable. Of course, as with the deliberate demotion of female deities in favour of male counterparts, the pagan snake, too, must be reviled.

It so occurs that Solomon, in one year, receives 666 talents of gold. Now back to the temple volume of 36000.

This 36000, too, can be given the king-lists numerical treatment, but it is also divisible by 18 and multiples thereof, all answers neatly rounded, with the exception of 54, a goddess-related figure of far-earlier origin than even Yahweh, a late-comer upon the scene. $36000 \div 54 = 666 \cdot 66666$. But they possessed no decimal system. Mayhap 666 shall suffice for the compilers of the Solomon's Temple story..

Without further ado I am about to bring the walls of Solomon's temple falling down. Well, at least to manageable levels figuratively, shall I say, or in belated fact?

Papa David, womanizer who ensured the death of a fellow whose wife he was giving the salacious eye, and with a hot desire to give her far more than that, instructed boy Solomon to have built a temple in accordance with details supplied.

Lacking almost all in materials required, such as timber, and the expertize of a skilled workforce, Solomon set about importing them.

And it came to pass that large amounts of cash, or bartered goods, were needed for so lavish a construction, the huge walls of which were to enclose a temple, the strangely-named House of the Pharoah's Daughter, Solomon's palace next door to it, a throne-room and a Hall of Columns.

One finds reason to ask, to where did that lot vanish to leave not a trace? Much lesser buildings stood for far-longer periods of time. Was Solomon's temple ever more than a dream?

Interesting is that within one year, near to talent-less (wealth-wise)

Solomon acquired six-hundred and three-score and six-talents of gold. So why the fuss over that Book of Revelations 666? Might that lack of evidence, that there was once a magnificent temple raised upon behalf of one King Solomon, be due to Herod who might have razed the whole edifice out of existence? Doubtful that, too.

From Sheba Solomon received, among other costly gifts, 120 talents in gold. One-hundred talents is equivalent of 11 pounds avoir du pois.

And King Solomon had made, for the temple, 200 targets of beaten gold, each target containing 600 shekels of gold. Thus 600 x 200 = 120,000.

120,000 is precisely divisible by 18.604651, the vital key-divisor by which the king-lists figures are made to give reason, and by 43. Let me remind you that 800 = 18.604651 x 43.

800 x 150 = 120,000. 150 is, of course, further divisible to a minor quantity.

However, by whichever the selected route all final answers must remain as whatever early astronomer-priestesses or priests wanted of them. After all, they had secrets to be keep free from the minds of any nosey member of their hoi polloi. In forbidden knowledge lay power. Official Secrets Acts of their day! Nothing changes!

There is also the statement that Solomon engaged all foreign inhabitants of Israel as slave-labour working to achieve his grand design. It was in truth forced labour. They numbered 153,600. I scratched my head! Here was a precise figure which was worthy of further investigation.

153,600 = 800 x 192. 192 is easily reduced to the lesser figure of one's choice. But it remains suited to the king-lists formula which formula has a lunar influence!

In one case, wherein Solomon makes an exchange of goods, he offers those who cut and supply the Lebonese timber, 20,000 each in measures beaten wheat, in barley, in baths of oil and in baths of wine.

This amounts to 4 x 20,000, or 80,000 in total. Since 80,000 is exactly divisible by 800 it is open to the same type of king-lists interpretation.

It might be that the biblical figures are rounded up or down to the nearest 100, Maybe! Maybe not! However, had that 153,600 temple-builders been made greater, or smaller, by 100 then the king-lists factor could not be applied with success. Nor would 153,800, nor would 153,500. Nor...900, nor.... 100, nor ....200, and so on.

No different than the politics of today, be they of Governments or Trades Unions, there was much secrecy among the temple's free-labour force, the professional element; know the correct sign or password and so much more is yours.

I can think of one semi-secret brotherhood, of today, that would be aware of this.

The two Pillars, Jaichim and Boaz to the temple fore, were of vast proportions, cast hollow, most-probably possible only in biblical terms of exaggeration.

And King Solomon caused to be manufactured temple furnishings, in both gold and in silver. They amount to the following quantities per item-

                10,000
                20,000
                40,000
                10,000
                80,000
                80,000
                60,000
                20,000

These quantities add to a total of 320,000. And with the 32 being a multiple of 8 it is clearly yet another of those king-lists type of enumeration.

Then come further quantities of temple furnishings in precious metals, dishes and the like.

$$80,000$$
$$8,000$$
$$60,000$$
$$20,000$$

These give a 168,000 total.

Both separately the 320,000 and 168,000 are immediately seen to be divisible by the king-lists factor of 18.604651 x 43, or 800, respective answers being 400 and 210. The same must apply when they are added together.

We now come to the Yahweh priesthood garments and other items of sacred necessity.

10,000 garments.
200,000 trumpets.
200,000 more garments.
40,000 musical instruments.

This lot would far outdo old Gabrielle in their blowing. This gives a grand total of 450,000. But this does not follow my king-lists numerical principles.

But to this add the 10,000 precious stones and we arrive at 460,000 now made undeniably divisible by 800 and all which that presents.

Throughout the Middle East, and generally throughout the Northern Hemisphere at least, matriarchalism prevailed; worship of the Goddess the norm, mere Man unaware of the *Magic* which enabled Woman to bear offspring or to periodically spill her blood without harm to herself. The Goddess must assuredly give her protection to their female counterparts.

Nor did Man have an awareness of a lunar influence in that spillage of blood. But Woman could count up to nine, thereby able to predict, well in advance, that she shall bear a child months ahead of the fact.

And Man failed to realize that he did play his part in making that possible whilst enjoying the company of his mate. Here was the Magic of the Goddess transmitted through the body of Woman.

Women were the gatherers of fruits, wild herbs and seeds and roots whilst men were the hunters of game. This enabled women alone to learn the secrets of herbal lore. More Magic! I wonder how often was a despised man removed by herbal poison?

So, after millennia, Man became so disenchanted with Woman's dominance, with gods invented, male to the core, and superior to any goddess.

It did not occur overnight. In fact it did not occur even during one-thousand years the transformation to monotheist patriarchalism. Long after Solomon, despite the earlier travails of Moses, many Hebrews continued to *Worship in High Places* in other words continued to pay homage to female deities.

Solomon, with many a wife of foreign extraction, late in life deserted Yahweh in favour of Astarte and company. He appears, here, to hedge his death-bed bets. *Solomon built an altar in a high place, upon a hill to the fore of Jerusalem, where incense was burnt and sacrifice made, for King Solomon went after Astoreth who is Astarte goddess of the Zidonians.* This biblical passage surely further reveals that Solomon's temple would have served for worship of both goddess and god, a case of choose the more convenient.

Within the temple was a chamber inside which was housed the Ark of the Covenant. The chamber measured 20 x 20 x 20 cubits.

20 cubed = 8000, which is 800 x 10.

Elsewhere is mention of the following temple artefacts

10,000 tables.

20,000 gold vessels.

40,000 silver vessels.

10.000 candlesticks.

80,000 pouring vessels.
100,000 gold vials.
80,000 gold dishes.
60,000 large basins in gold.
20,000 measures.
These quantities add up to 420,000, another multiple of 800.

Masons

Phoenician, Master Mason, Hiram Abiff, was he who alone had sufficient knowledge to oversee all aspects of construction on Solomon's Temple. Only he knew the secret of casting the rather huge Jaichim and Boaz pillars in bronze, albeit that they were hollow and said to be 18 cubits in height, with a circumference of 3.8 cubits, a lot of bronze, a costly lot. And their thickness was of 4 fingers, those round walls.

Externally polished, set before so magnificent a temple, reflecting bright sunlight they would have made a pair of blinding beacons seen from afar.

And we must not overlook that which they called The Great Sea.

The Great Sea was a huge bowl set upon feet. It contained water whereby to purify the hands and feet of priests.

The rim of this bronze bowl stood at 10 cubits above floor-level, supported by 12 feet in the form of oxen, and all in bronze.

There is, too, the bronze laver which stood upon 4 wheels, this laver another huge bowl with a diameter of 4 cubits, the whole standing upward of 4 cubits. Whatever the accumulated weight of these bowls they would have been worth one quarter of that weight of gold. Quite a skilful mason was Hiram Abiff, it would seem.

There remains, however, a mystery surrounding the sudden death of that superlative mason, that master craftsman without equal.

Hiram Abiff was from Tyre, a city of Heathens, unapproved by Hebrew Yahweh. But to Solomon, who creates High Places for worship of heathen deities, quite acceptable in the sense of business, at least. Similar things are accepted today when so-called democracies do unashamed trade with dictatorships.

From the Freemasonic Brotherhood, of today, comes the legend that

Hiram Abiff was confronted by three of his apprentices, this shortly after his completion of work for Solomon, and within the temple-walls, even then a sacrosanct haven, one supposes. They, the trio of apprentices, demanded that their employer reveal to them the secret signs and passwords used by senior members of the workforce in order that they may, too, use them to their own advantage.

Hiram refused to comply with his apprentices' demands and, during his endeavours to escape, was caught and murdered by them, within the temple, near to the entrance-doors, then taken outside to be buried among local hills.

All of the above occurred after night-fall. And this raises questions.

The temple is complete, it's entrance-doors locked against thieves and unclean persons, the priesthood gone home. Only chosen members, among priestly officials, would be in a position to unlock those doors. Why then are three apprentices still inside the temple-walls? Why indeed shall Hiram linger there with nothing more required of him? How were three apprentices able to carry a corpse outside and make for the hills, all undetected? Did they make use of some secret passage? And, with all of that secrecy, who left a record of so ghastly an affair? Not apprentices wishing to escape justice! If those villains knew of a secret-passage then it was no secret.

During construction of the temple Hiram Abiff, in his position of Master Mason, could not be but aware of any secrets contained within it's erection requirements, and would have detected any element that seemed to indicate that all was not orientated in line with strict observance in worship of monotheistic Yahweh.

It appears that fellow-masons found Hiram's dead-body at a *High Place,* biblical terminology for heathen centres of worship and sacrifice to older-than Yahweh deities. And this particular High Place faced Jerusalem. Might it be that very same which was so-closely associated with Solomon?

The second Creation myth provides description of an attempt to banish goddess-worship from throughout the whole of Israel. By the reign of Solomon the attempts continued. Our Eve is derived from Hebrew Hiwwa, itself rooted in Hittite Goddess Herwa.

The Golden Calf and other such sacrifices would be conducted at other High Places, too.

Assuming that Hiram discovered that the Temple to Solomon served not only Yahweh, but also Astoreth, then Solomon might have reason to keep the master-mason's lips closed forever, in order to maintain that secret of subterfuge in spiritual double-dealing.

From legend come instances of some heroe's head buried at the approaches to a city, placed there **to** ward evil influences from entering the metropolis. Here, in a defilement of a sacred temple by an act of murder, can it be that, beneath the surface, is a portrayal of a human sacrifice in the form of Hiram Abiff, buried to overlook King Solomon's Temple?

One biblical prophet, Ahizah, did foretell (after the event?) that Solomon would be stripped of royal control of Israel, Jerusalem alone remaining under his jurisdiction, this due to the fact that the king worshipped Astarte/Ashtoreth, a goddess and foreign at that.

During ensuing years Hebrews persisted in building groves and images in high places-upon every hill.

And there were Sodomites in the land, and they did according to all abominations of the Nations that the Lord cast out before the Children Of Israel.

Something of an unholy bunch were those Hebrews, cruel, too, if we are to believe biblical sources. Yahweh's judgement, of who shall be the Chosen People, was not infallible, after all.

Four centuries pass, following the death of Solomon, the task of re-building his temple, destroyed by invading armies, is begun.

They intrigue me, the details relating to a refurbished temple.

50 chargers in gold.
500 chargers of silver.
40 Thericlean cups in gold.
500 Thericlean cups in silver.
50 Bastons in gold.
500 Bastons in silver.
30 Drinking vessels in gold.
300 Drinking vessels in silver.
30 vials in gold.
2400 vials in silver.
1000 other vessels.

The above quantities total 5,400. But are these figures forced, I wonder?

There are three instances wherein silver vessels are 10 times larger than for their gold equivalents. However, although there are 40 Therilean cups in gold here, the rule does not apply for their equivalent in silver is 500 and not 400. Apart from that the vials in gold are 30 whilst there are 80 times that in silver. And what of that 1,000 *other* vessels?

To this re-built temple King Cyrus sent those costly gifts but, even so, in number and value, they are nowhere close to the lavishness of Solomon's temple accessories. They do, nonetheless, give us a total of 5400.

Take John Michell's temple construction figure of 1080; 5400 divided by this equals 5.

At last, in the year 516 BC., in March if you wish, the temple to Solomon is finally re-built along lesser dimensions of 20 x 20 x 10 cubits. This gives a volume reduction of 4000, against the former 36000.

Naturally, 4000 is divisible by the king-lists lunar factor of 800, another reduction to 5.

There remain the apologists for the fall of Solomon from Yahweh grace; *his women had led him astray.* But what should one expect from a monotheist bunch of priestly misogynistic sodomites?

More dimensions, of interest, come from the words of Josephus. They are related to the Herodian temple construction and are 25 x 8 x 12 cubits. These figures give a total of 2400, clearly divisible by the king-lists, lunar- associated 800, the minimum reduction-figure being 3.

If there never was an original temple built upon behalf of King Solomon, therefore no Hiram Abiff, upon what do the Freemasons of today base their origins?

Fundamental to Templar wealth was ownership of property. And, with property, comes land upon which to erect temples for the Order.

I have pondered deeply upon why legendary, and huge spans of time, from widely-dispersed sources in the Northern Hemisphere, all share the same method of mathematical reduction to reach fundamental numerical values, and I find no reason to doubt that a diversity of able astronomers, from bygone days, made serious study of both lunar and solar cycles, the former set against the latter as a constant. Yet, although the same mathematics is concealed within the holes to a much greater extent than stones at Stonehenge, the same interests in the night-skies must have prevailed at the megalithic site.

Today a study of personal bank-balances is preferred.

If all of those numerical values, which relate with the Temple of Solomon accounts, are accepted as being merely some form of idiosyncratic fairy-tale, then how strong, or feeble, the roots of Freemasonry. With so many co-incidences of figures that are divisible by 43 x 18.604652, (800) there must be reason behind them, that of someone who treats them like magic numbers. Which, perhaps they were in some manner.

They called their Brotherhood, The Order of the Temple of Solomon, did the Knights Templar, they who, from the *heathen* Moslem, learnt of the intricacies of mathematical Pi. From the same much-maligned people they learnt of the use of refined geometric principals and how to put them to use, such as in the superb construction of the Dome of the Rock in Jerusalem, by Moslem architects during the 7th century AD. Some headstones, within Templar cemeteries, continue to show representations of the simple tools belov-ed insignia of today's Freemasons.

Without need of calculation of weights and measure my engineering background tells me that, for instance, the huge bowl in bronze, the Great Sea laver set upon 12 feet, and standing at 10 cubits in height, that is in the general region of 15-feet English, would present an impossible task in the casting. As would the pillars, Jaichim and Boaz. What is more, the cost would have been monumental.

Something of a climb that, 10-cubits (15-feet) to take a bath!

And Goddess Lilith sent hand-maidens to assist Yahweh with his Creation-bit.

I previously referred to John Michel's figure of 1080 which can be seen in relation to quantities of bricks required for the building of fire-surrounds within Indian sacred temples, even the temples themselves. 108 = 2 x 54, the 54 being associated with worship of goddesses, one of those magic-numbers of yore. In fact when divided into 25,920, that figure, Precession of the Equinoxes, beloved of *horrorscopelogists*, Aquarius and all of that, 108 gives an answer that happens to be 240, in itself an interesting numerical value with a final reduction of 3, perhaps indicative of the Triple Goddess, of whom Artemis, as Maiden-Virgin, her colour white, was one.

Upon the Trail of Arthur and Clovis 1.

There arise occasions when someone exclaims, 'I swear I left it (or dropped it) here!' perhaps an ear-clip or small screw essential to the re-assembly of some favoured, personal item. Then, yards from the designated area of search with magnifying glass, or magnet (that has no attraction for things in brass,) eagle-eyed little Jenny enquires, 'Is this what you're looking for?' assuming that the family dog has not already inadvertently carried out said object into the garden with it stuck between the pads of a paw. For me the legendary Arthur represents such a misplaced object.

Within our shores no Camelot, nor associated points of possible interest to Arthurians in the objective sense, has been found, no magical Merlin's crystal cave discovered concealed beneath centuries of obscuring vine and belladonna intermingled with creeping elements of wishful thought and superstitious imagination.

No search for the intangible should ever be mounted without first a study of evidence stripped of it's tantalizing gloss. The more that one investigates Arthur the more bemused does one become. To the open mind, nonetheless, there exists a feint suggestion, a thread common to most variations on original Arthurian themes, that should not be overlooked.

In his 'History of the Kings of England' William of Malmesbury considers Arthur to be in reality, a glorious hero, and not a character of pure fable. Many more, since the time of William, have come to believe in a flesh and blood Arthur, a figure worthy of meritorious acclaim. The same can be said of latter-day romanticizers.

How much is to be accepted as truth in the exaggerated words of Geoffrey of Monmouth, self-proclaimed historian?

Embroidery of word is the mark of poets. It is exploited to an extreme by Geoffrey, and other authors of later years, men of the lustrous pen wielded with a mystifying flourish that distracts and misleads. It is that verbal mist of perplexing phraseology that must be removed when attempting to separate fact from fiction, if indeed any fact exists.

In British tradition Arthur is Celtic through and through. He is bold, he is reckless. He signifies the courage of a Celtic chieftain when charging into battle. He also reflects the later trappings that surround mediaeval courts, brave knight in burnished armour, swaying plume in his helm, chivalrous, courteous, women held in high esteem. Troubadours, when speaking of Arthur, clothe him with a magical quality, a glamour of near to sacredness. Arthur, in fact, becomes a too-good-to-be-true character.

Those famous Twelve Battles, no matter how refined the microscope of investigation, leave us not one solid fact by which to confirm that they ever took place. Where, then, did that ultra-brave band of Celtic freedom-fighters, led by Arthur, spill so much of their own and that of a Saxon enemy's gore?

We find vestiges of Arthur of the British fifth-century, extended by centuries more until we encounter the Templar Knights. Arthur is in Wales, Cornwall, Brittany, the Pyrenees Mountains, Italy and even further afield. No doubt some Yank will prove that Arthur beat Columbus in reaching the New World. What then of original sources claimed by Mallory, Chrétien de Troyes, and many another exponent of the Grail Mystery? Who knows?

Where should one go in search of Camelot, Avalon, Arthur's grave, his magic Excalibur, his Guinevere?

It is the habit of poets to be enigmatic in order to heighten the air of mystique, as did Arthurian romancers.

Only with some understanding of earlier religious practices in vogue across the whole European continent, and the accompanying folklore, is it possible to glean an inkling of what could prove to be that mysterious source-material of which Chrétien makes claim. Distributed throughout the romances are slender clues which serve to present a path to be taken when in pursuit of Arthur's roots.

It was essential that writers of romances should glorify an Arthur who is a Christian. It would have been perilous for them to do otherwise for, in the Church of Rome, a heathen Celt, no matter how exalted to the plebeian of mind, was fuel for the fires of Hell. And the Grail, whatever it may be, had to be dressed in a Christian overcoat, too. But was that grail some three-dimensional object or some esoteric phantom?

In relation to folklore, legend and myth, it is important to take note of the seemingly insignificant. This may appear in personal or place-name, in the paraphernalia of rite and ritual, in mention of certain colours, in heraldic components, in strange beasts, and not so strange. The Stag may well represent the human soul. Such animals as Roebuck, Bear, Hound and Hart are rarely included free of symbolic meaning.

Geoffrey of Monmouth, quite appropriately, tells of a Bear that appears in Arthur's nightmares.

From romance to romance the hero's name undergoes change. He is Arthur; he is Percival; he is Parzival; he is Lohengrin.

Sir Thomas Mallory gives a vivid picture of his particular Arthur, a picture upon which more than one film has been based, although their settings are far more indicative of a later era.

Perhaps I appear to be far too much the cynic in my judgement of the authenticity of tales relating to Arthur, or maybe not. I, however, chose to work upon the assumption that Arthur never existed in the form that reaches down to us. Rather than seek a Camelot that lies here, an Avalon that lies there, I selected to broaden my sphere of investigation, giving free-rein to the direction that some word or phrase, or intuition might trigger.

To employ my lost object analogy, I sought evidence which might rest far from the central sphere which the romances imply, that is both geographically and historically. Perhaps that Grail would prove to be the most unholy of objects.

Both place and personal names, involving the Grail - family, show much imagination on the part of authors. Some of them depict a strong Celtic influence. And one of Arthur's Continental residences was at a place called CARDUEIL.

I took a closer look at the name CARDUEIL. Remove the IL and one has CARDUE. The Celtic word for BLACK is DUE. In like fashion Celtic CAR means FORT. It was the Celtic habit to place the noun before the descriptive word. So FORT BLACK becomes BLACK FORT for us. I know of a BLACK FORT. It lies in south-western France not so far from the Pyrenees where they say that Arthur made an appearance. This is Pech CARDOU, Cardou Peak. And Celts once occupied that region. It is to this same region that Clovis 1 fought a real Battle with the Visigoths. The Knights Templar also held a strong presence in that very same vicinity. Which brings us the Wolfram von Eschenbach.

Wolfram, yet another to enchant readers with his tale of Parzival, broadens the romance with introduction of Templar knights. In his accurate description of Templar fighting techniques, and the weaponry used, Wolfram either made a close study of the knights in action or was himself a former Knight of the Temple. Whilst Chrètien de Troyes' Grail is more a magical dish, never holy, the pen of Wolfram makes it both holy and miraculous.

Like Chrètien, Wolfram makes mention of a king, the former being the Fisher King, a figure who is lamed, the latter is described as being wounded between the thighs.

The numbers of heroes, who are severely wounded in one fashion or another, are somewhat numerous throughout the realms of legend.

Welsh Bran and Greek Achilles each are wounded in the heel. Arthur, of course, is wounded. Beware the word lamed, in this context! It implies ritual wounding by removal of the genitals, even a sacrificial death.

When first coming across mention of the Fisher King, I became intrigued by the fact that he was lamed. Here was a possible clue worth further examination.

Single-handed combat is also suggestive of a time when tanist fought the Goddess's surrogate for his title and position, a regular such ritual from the past.

Wolfram reveals the original source from which he compiled his work, material written in Arabic, he remarks, written by a heathen Jew by the name of Flegetanis, However, this Flegetanis fellow *'Knew the starry script, could read the heavens high, how the stars roll on their courses, how they circle the silent sky. And the time when wandering ends, and the life and lot of men. He read the stars and strange secrets he saw'*.

So Flegetanis is both astronomer and astrologer, a learned man who can write and calculate heavenly cycles.

Wolfram makes his Flegetanis both a Jew and a heathen, too. The Church would more than frown upon a heathen being alloted so cultured a status. It is accepted, nevertheless, that Wolfram drew upon a broad spectrum of sources when creating his romance. He was writing at a time when Rome was in conflict with the Cathars in the Languedoc of Gaul, and of magic and esoteric traditions. yet he is deliberate in his use of opposites, as in black versus white. In his work one may observe a battle between good and evil, too. I do not see him as a moralist for he appears to take the central path.

In Quest de San Graal a date is given, that of 487 AD, which same date has significance in that only one year earlier Clovis 1 had already established the first stage in his empire building. This is the Clovis with the sobriquet of Bear, the very king who has become, for some, identified with Arthur.

When Clovis arrived in the region of the Franco-Belge Ardennes he was pagan as any monarch could be. That forest, where Cults of the Bear had existed, probably from an early Neolithic era, was a most appropriate spot for him in which to settle .

At around that same date Arthur comes to us as a champion of Christendom.

Like Arthur, but in reality, Clovis fought a number of battles, losing none. At Soissons he engaged and defeated the Roman army, thus taking for himself the title, King of the Romans. Asterix never quite went that far.

Ten years on, when fighting the Visigoths, Clovis vowed to become a Christian if the battle went in his favour.

Alaric, Visigoth king, seeing defeat of his army as being inevitable, escaped the fray. Clovis was duly baptised into the Christian faith upon Christmas-day 496 AD.

A further ten years passed and Clovis, in good old Arthurian fashion, slew Alaric in single combat, the remaining Visigoths retreating to Rennes le Château in the Aude region of the French Languedoc, having lost an empire straddling the Pyrenees right into Spain proper. Arthur is said to have been to the Pyrenees.

Merovingian (to which family Clovis belonged) priest-kings, famous for their long hair, claimed descent from Troy. They also, through Childeric, father of Clovis, adopted the Lily of the Valley as a family emblem, the emblem of King David. This adoption is in line with Merovingian claims to the Holy Land and bordering territories.

Is it coincidence that Clovis had his Guenevere, virgin-heroine pre-dating Jeanne d'Arc?

The Bear element in successive Merovingian kings remains mindful of Arthur as Bear-man. For a thousand years Celts had been crossing the Channel from north-eastern France and Belgium, as well as Brittany. I wonder did Clovis of the Ardennes thus acquaint himself with Celtic tales of Arthurian-type, Celtic Heroes?

However, I have reason to waste no time in proving any firm connection between an actual Clovis and a mythical Arthur, just as I have equal reason to look for Arthur in more unlikely places.

As a matter of possible interest Clovis fought battles outside of France prior to making war within the Frankish realm, itself. Here he took part in seven battles, those of Soissons, Paris, Rheims, Troyes, Amiens, Carcassonne and Toulouse. Is it any wonder that so stalwart a fighting man be compared with Arthur?

Across Western Europe the power of Rome had weakened. If it was to combat the growing strength of the Greek Orthodox, centred on Constantinople, something drastic was needed. To such an end it granted Clovis the title of Novus Constantinus, New Constantine, a second Emperor of the Holy Roman Empire. With his newly-born status Clovis was given permission to reign, but not to politically govern his expanded territory. As to any crowning ceremony there was no need for a man already recognized as king.

And Clovis employed the sword, when required, in spreading the faith of his benign masters.

In Merovingian custom, when he died the empire of Clovis was divided between his four sons. This naturally reduced the power of each kingdom's rulers often at loggerheads, one with another.

By employment of plots and lies Merovingian power was broken by the Church, its promises to Clovis openly disregarded, some male members of the dynasty forced to flee to England and Ireland. One among them, five years of age Prince Dagobert, was abducted by the Mayor of the Palace who planned to install his own son upon the throne. By one means or another Prince Dagobert was assisted in his reaching a monastery in Ireland, close to Dublin. Here he was educated and grew up. In 664 AD Dagobert married a Celtic princess. His Matilde died six years later when giving birth to their third daughter. In 671 AD Dagobert married for a second time, his new wife being Giselle de Razés She was niece to a Visigoth king, two important bloodlines intermingled.

Rennes le Château, the heavily-fortified hilltop village to which the Visigoths retreated from an unstoppable onslaught by the army of Clovis, was formerly known as the Rhédae, in the district of the Razés. Rhédae went through a change in name to become the Rennes le Château of today. It was here, at Rhédae, that Dagobert married Giselles de Razés.

Dagobert, wasted little time in establishing himself lord of a large area of north-eastern France, that of the Ardennes where, two centuries previously, his ancestor, Clovis had ruled supreme. At that time, and for centuries yet to come, Cults of the Bear flourished in the Ardennes.

Surrounded by envious neighbours Rome, far from pleased with Dagobert's quite righteous antipathy toward it, when recalling those broken promises made to his ancestor, put the Merovingian in great danger on a number of fronts.

There is reason to be suspicious of the manner of Dagobert's death by murderous hand. It occurred on December the 23rd. 679 AD., when someone forced a lance through the eye of a sleeping king, beside a stream during a hunt in the Forest of Woivres, a sacred forest mindful of Arthur's Forest of Broceliande in Brittany. William 11, Rufus and king of England, also met a suspicious death, inside a forest, too; the New forest.

Rome gave support to the assassins of Dagobert. But, with December the 23rd being so close to the day of the winter solstice, one wonders if the date was deliberately chosen by the slayers, for the purpose of ritual sacrifice?

Dagobert left a son by Giselle de Razés, Sigisbert who became

Count of Razés, yet another in that line of long-haired monarchs who believed in magical properties present in long hair, such as gave Samson his strength.

That the Merovingians claimed descent from Troy, and frequently adopted a Bear diminutive to accompany a king's name, provides reason to examine the Bear a little more closely.

The City of Troy lies at no great distance from Greek Arcadia where Cults of the Bear paid tribute to Artemis with whom the beast is closely associated, just as she also ruled in the Forest of the Ardennes under the guise of Arduina for centuries long after the death of Clovis I, in fact well into the 14th century of our era.

History often throws up an incident which defies logical interpretation. There is another that involves Dagobert, murdered, Rome failing to condemn the killers to eternal damnation.

While people became more knowledgeable, with the passage of time, far less likely to fall for superstitious rantings from the world of the celebrity-seekers, the Church of Rome faced circumstances that made it necessary to behave with increasing circumspection when deliberating upon the question of should this or that individual deserve canonization, or should many an apparent miracle be accepted as such, when it may well be due to some quirk of Nature, freak atmospheric conditions, of hallucination or misrepresentation by persons all too eager to claim sight of some vision relating to one of the divine beings with which their religious teachings made them over-familiar. Hysteria among religious fanatics was once quite common given suitable circumstances.

The Virgin appears to some young and excitable girl, her description of the apparition making her Lady, White-European young and slender, with a dress of pale-blue trimmed in gold, the very image to be found in a child's religious picture-book, or local church statue. A more true to life description would surely be appropriate with a Virgin of Eastern

Mediterranean colouring of the flesh, and desert garb. It must be very difficult, when faced with yet another guaranteed source of revenue, to deny it's veracity.

The Church was as much responsible for the murder of Joan of Arc as was Henry V1. The Church, however, finally recognized its error by canonizing Joan.

Dagobert was not left overlong in peace. He was first buried in the royal chapel at Rheims. A couple of centuries later he was re-interred at a church dedicated to his name, that of Saint Dagobert, an apparent act of guilty conscience smoothing.

In the eyes of ordinary people Dagobert becomes a hero with his own personal feast-day, that of December 23rd.

Then a local nobleman commandeered the Church of St. Dagobert.

Come the year 1093 Godfroi de Bouillon brings along a siege-army bent upon returning the St. Dagobert church to its rightful protector, the Abbey of Gorse. That was in the year 1093 AD. Wolfram von Eschenbach introduced a Templar element to his tale of Parzival. In 1099 AD, six years after his affair with the St. Dagobert church, Godfroi de Bouillon captured Jerusalem in company with other nobles, amongst whom were those claiming to be of the Merovingian bloodline, with the inclusion of Godfroi himself, and one Blanchefort of particular interest, a Blanchefort from Rennes le Château in the French Languedoc.

It matters little, that intrigue and machinations against the earlier Merovingian dynasty, by which the Carolingians usurped the crown. Although the murder of Dagobert 11 signalled the end of Merovingian rule, his son, Sigisbert IV, Count of Razés, simply disappears from the pages of history. . Nevertheless, one authority gives evidence that this Sigisbert did take on titles and position during the year 681 AD, and on record is one Sigisbert, Count of the Rhédae, who founded a monastery in 718 AD, which would occur during the possible lifetime of Sigibert IV, also known as Prince Ursus. It requires no furrowing of the brow to equate Ursus with that old Bear.

It is well documented that an independent princedom, or kingdom, continued in existence one century later than 718 AD. And the likelihood is that its ruler was of the Merovingian/Visigoth bloodline.

Not until the Albigensian, so-called Crusade, when the Church of Rome displayed a pitiless, blood-thirsty role in the matter, that an autonomous Languedoc, where sits the Rhédae, Razés, or Rennes le Château of today, fell into French hands as opposed to that of Merovingian Franks.

Wolfram von Eschenbach places his Grail family in the Pyrenees Mountains where Guillem de Gellone ruled, another distinguished battler, a second Clovis but warring on behalf of Carolingian Charlemagne.

Assuming a continuation of the Merovingian bloodline through Sigisbert 1V and Guillem de Gellone, it reaches out to embrace the Duchies of Brittany and Aquitaine.

In the year 999 AD Godfroi de Bouillon went on to capture Jerusalem before returning the Church of St. Dagobert back under the authority of the Abbey of Gorse. He made his brother, Baudouin, Patriarch of the Holy City, a man claiming Merovingian blood, now installed as King of the Holy Land, as his ancestors asserted to be their right.

On an earlier page I omitted to write that Wolfram states that a certain Kyot discovered the manuscript worded in Arabic, in the town of Spanish Toledo. But it is Wolfram who places the Grail castle in the Pyrenees. He also introduces a Duchess of Brabant late in his tale. Brabant is a province of Belgium, lying not so far distant from the Ardennes Forest, where Clovis 1 once reigned. In fact the whole of Belgium came into his kingdom. Since Clovis went warring in the Pyrenees, too, where lies the Grail Castle, what is Wolfram telling us beneath the surface? Is his Arthurian style of romance designed with an obscured intention to promote the Merovingians as rightful heirs to the throne of France? He also involves the Templars at some length, Templars who showed favour to the Catharis of Languedoc, and, as many a ruined castle and château reveals, once settled in some strength in the general vicinity of the Razés and Rennes le Château guarding the gateway south to The Mediterranean Sea and Perpignan.

When, years ago, I first took a serious interest in myth, legend and mystery from the past, I could not foresee a network of research paths that would lead me ever further afield, broadening out to encompass a time before the coming of recorded history in print, and most of the European Continent as well as part of Asia Minor. Why was it that I often found myself confronted by the Bear element in association with characters from legend and myth?

Although not well-acquainted with the subject I am aware that, from time immemorial, Bear-cults existed right across the European continent into Eurasia, as no other single animal ever was heralded so widely. It might be that such reverence was due to the beast's power of physique, it"s fearlessness, its speed of movement across the terrain although outwardly an ungainly animal. Perhaps the fact that it often stood upon two legs like human beings, gave it cause for admiration.

A Further Look for Atlantis.

The US clairvoyant, Edgar Cayce, claimed that Atlantis was due to rise from out of the sea in the year 1968/9. It did not come about. It was to reappear off the Bahamas in the Atlantic Ocean, not far from the coast of Florida. Cayce also claimed that Atlanteans were technically as advanced as are we. If that were so then surely they would have possessed instruments to give them at least enough warning of an impending earthquake for them to have made some sort of preparations for their Big Bang. Or could it be that the Atlanteans, like so many people of our times, chose to stay at home when their cities were being turned into infernoes by incendiary bombing, the it-will-never- happen- to-us types?

Nevertheless, underwater explorations have indicated the presence of huge blocks of stone in relatively-shallow waters off Bimini in the Bahamas. Yet this locality lies far distant from central Atlantic climes where most interested parties place Plato's Atlantis. There are other regions, around the World, where similar, apparently man-made walls and thoroughfares lie in shallow water like long-lost cities near to major coastlines.

Writers use the Atlantis theme to explain similarities in early cultures on both sides of the Atlantic Ocean, pyramids in both Egypt and Latin America, sun-worship and the like, flora and fauna that are the same. But Continental Drift accounts for the latter whilst the former requires further exploration.

When it was observed that blue-tits, in the UK, learnt how to peck holes through milk bottle tops, to get to the cream beneath, at the very same time that their cousins were doing precisely the same in Australia, why should not humans behave in similar fasion?

However, Greeks of Old, and others were sea-faring nations who must be credited with much versatility in the art of building wonderful ships. Irish legend tells of invasions of that country, three to four thousand years in the past. The invaders, according to Robert Graves' exceptional reconstruction of those stories, came from the Aegean, some by land, others by sea in doing so forced to go outside the Pillars of Heracles (Hercules).

So why should some of those early sailors not have, by accident or to see what lay beyond the Atlantic Ocean's western horizon, found themselves caught in the Gulf Stream's westerly sweep en route to the Gulf of Mexico and, perhaps returning home to Europe on it's north-easterly path? There are those who will always insist that Columbus did it first.

Poseidon and his City of Atlantis came to the attention of another US citizen, one Ignatius Donnelly, 1831- 1901 who considered Plato's Atlantis to be a fact of history.

In that he may be correct in a different time-scale. He promulgated that the Phoenician alphabet was rooted in that of Atlantis. He found cultural parallels between east and west, relative to the Atlantic Ocean. But with the passage of time theories such as those of Cayce ,without archaeological proof to back them, have a habit of getting themselves blown sky- high.

Robert Graves, as learned a researcher as any into the past, states that the Phoenician alphabet has it's source in an earlier Cretan-influenced Egyptian counterpart. Furthermore, Phoenicians, Greeks, Irish, Vikings, you name them, are all too recent culturally if Plato is to be believed.

Nevertheless, all of those named, and a few others including the Bretons, might possibly have 'Discovered the Americas'. After all, Breton sailors wore trousers made of a cloth invented in France, the same cloth of which Levy made his Jeans. Of such minor incidents do cultural elements spread abroad. Poseidon, God of Seas and

Earthquakes - I would have expected Thunder-balls Zeus to be a better contender for the Earthquake title, he the god who had ten sons comprising five sets of twins that he begat through services rendered by Cleito, a human female with whom he fell in love. Atlantis City was built around the hill where Cleito dwelt. This city was formed of concentric rings of alternating water and land, seven in all if one includes Cleito's hill at the centre. It is mindful of the week of seven days and the seven gods so presented with associated planets.

Heinrich Schliemann, *a mere amateur archaeologist*, found the remains of an ancient city at Hissalik in northern Turkey, Homer's Troy no less, one of a number by the name rebuilt after destruction by war, earthquake and plague et cetera. Here was proof, if needed, that Greek myths should be taken seriously. They do reflect historical truths beneath the embellishment. And not only Greek myths.

The City of Troy, long thought to be a figment of Homer's brilliant imagination, was proven to be a reality. So what of Plato's Atlantis, fact or fiction? If fact it remains to be discovered.

There is much in Plato's dialogue that I consider to be a narrator's gloss added to bring life to the tale in order that an audience does not drift into sleep. I will ignore that superfluous decoration and select points overlooked by other investigators with pet theories to prove.

The Egyptian priest informs Solon that, *at the head of the Egyptian Delta, where the river divides, is a certain district called Sais, and is the city from which King Amasis was sprung. And the citizens have a deity who is their foundress. She is called, in the Egyptian tongue, Neith which is asserted to be the same as she whom the Hellenes called Athene.*

Here is mention of Athene, she who came into competition with Poseidon in order to prove which of them could create something that was the more beneficial to the people of Earth. Please keep that in mind.

'She (Athene) founded your city of Athens 1000 years before our's (Sais) .... the constitution of which is set down in sacred registers as 8000 years old. As touching the citizens (Athenians) of 9000 years ago I will briefly inform you of their laws'.

And there was an island situated in front of the straits which you call the Columns of Heracles.

Many researchers accept that Atlantis was situated more or less in mid-Atlantic. The Egyptian priest is saying that the island stood in front of the Pillars of Heracles (Hercules). From the viewpoint of an Egyptian on home territory I would expect 'in front' to relate to his side of the Pillars of Heracles/, nearer to himself on Mediterranean shores rather than the Atlantic side. That piece about mud in the ocean, and distant continents I choose to look at as though they are decorative additions to the basic story. When others, wishing to prove an hypothesis, take only that which will serve their purpose, why not I? Again from the mouth of an Egyptian priest...

But afterwards there occurred violent earthquakes and floods...

And the island of Atlantis disappeared beneath the sea.

There is a passage from Plato's dialogue which tells of people fleeing inside the Pillars of Heracles. Can this mean from the Atlantic to the inside of the straits or, being already on the Mediterranean side, they just fled for their lives in whichever direction it suited them to take?

Poseidon, in competition with Athene, brought forth a natural spring of salt-water. Athene, she being *The Wise*, caused a mature olive tree to come into a flourishing being. That lady was adjudged the winner. And rightly so!

In terms of fundamental usefulness, to it's inhabitants, Plato's Atlantis had an abundance of both hot and cold springs of water. He also reveals that stones, employed in the construction of city buildings, palaces and temples were white, red and black in colour. Greek temples to the lunar-goddess, in triad form, would have included elements of white, red and black in adornments, probably in the stones used. White represented the goddess in Virgin-maiden aspect, whilst red would signify her nubile maturity, black the old-woman as Wise Crone.

Upon the map of the Aude region, one may observe the peaks, Roc Blanc, Roque Rouge and Roque Nègre. In English the rocks, white, red and black!

A Poseidon spring of salt; the French verb, to salt, is Saler, with appropriate Sal derivatives. Seven kilometres to south-east of Rennes les Bains is Fontaine Salée, the salt spring that feeds the River Sals, a most fitting name. We are here concerned with a vicinity of France which lies upon the same latitude as an area of Ancient Greece with similar terrain features. Atlantis had its mountains, too.

In his masterly reconstruction of Greek myths and, especially various traditions within these our Isles, Robert Graves tells of Welsh legend referring to heavy seas breaking through sea-walls to inundate sixteen cities. Other *'Lost Atlantis'* are to be found in sites lost to the seas,, Irish Hy Brasil, The Breton City of *Ys,* the Cornish Land of Lyonesse, French Isle Verte and Portugese Ilha Verde, all of them in the far-west, European coastlines. I am forced to wonder if all of these catastrophes actually occurred, all within the same time-setting, as a result of some colossal earthquake during a distant past. One must never deride folk-memory as being the stuff of fairy tales; just as ancient myth all too often conceals a kernel of historic truth.

For an earthquake to sink Irish Hy Brasil, and those other locations mentioned above, it must have been reasonably localized, perhaps in Western Europe.

Graves asks what if the Egyptian priest informed Solon that when the Atlantis disaster took place survivors fled beyond the Pillars of Heracles, meaning from inside the Mediterranean. He goes further. But first I must admit that I am not then conversant with his Diodorus

Siculus a man who would make pleasant company for the likes of Plutarch, Finder and Strabo.

Through the pen of Diodorus Siculus Graves relates, *'In the country of the Atlantians lived a most civilized people, westward beyond Lake Tritonis'*.

Lake Tritonis is in Libya, once a vast lake of fresh water, now reduced to little more than salt marshes.

Substitute the rivers Blanque and Sals, which both share a confluence a little to south of Rennes les Bains, for Plato's canals at Atlantis, add to that an abundance of hot and cold springs, equivalent to the Greek's account, and the similarities grow. In the region of Languedoc is a number of villages and towns whose name has the suffix Bains (Baths), fed by natural springs of water, Alet les Bains, for instance.

To the north-west of Rennes les Bains two names are to be seen on the map. They are Camp Grand (Great camp) and les Capitelles, which last I am unable to translate but I sense that it reflects something outstanding architecturally. They lie not far too north of the River Sals' western sweep.

Les Capitelles consist of a vast array of huge walls built of stones held in place by their own weights, remains, one might think, of ruins such as those of Troy. They remind others of early Mycenaean structures, as do the photographs of them remind me. Mycenae, I believe, lay at the same latitude.

Before the arrival of Roman legions in the area Celts inhabited the landscape. Boudet's menhirs indicate an earlier culture than that of the Celts. Pre-Hellenic Greeks penetrated Western Europe, to set up colonies along the northern Mediterranean shores. Celts awarded them rights of passage on the Continent. Greeks landed at Gades, today's Spanish Cadiz, just outside the Pillars of Heracles. They set foot at Nice and Marseilles not any great distance from the Aude region at the Mediterranean end of the Pyrenees Range. That chain of mountains, running almost east to west, would surely have been seen to be on fire on a clear evening at sunset, particularly at the equinoxes. Pyrrha means, in full, fiery-red. And that it how the range assumed it's Greek name.

'And it is said that, as the result of a series of earthquakes, the seas engulfed Lake Tritonis.' Those earthquakes are, therefore, to be placed somewhere in the region of the Mediterranean Sea. Since Diodorus is also saying that the Atlantians lived to west of Lake Tritonis they would appear to dwell, when taking into account their name, towards the Atlantic coast of North Africa, lying to south of the Pillars of Heracles.

The two Rennes, le Château and les Bains, rest not far inland from the Mediterranean coastline, at no great distance from the Straits of Gibraltar and the Pillars of Hercules, as they are known to us.

Hot thermal springs are created by heat from the Earth's core, such as are to be found in earthquake zones.

Hot-water springs form naturally in the region of the Aude.

One therefore assumes that the Earth's crust is somewhat thinner there than on average. A further factor supports volcanic implications in that vicinity: there is that most revealing name of Roque Fumade-*Smoking Rock*, not the only equally-suggestive name to be found there.

I, myself, suspect that Plato, as raconteur, was employing exaggeration and invention to hold his audience's attention all the better. Drawing upon older tradition he gave his story his own modifications to make it the more exciting. He was, after all, a professional at his task.

So far as I am aware no in-depth study has been mounted by archaeologists in that area of France. Could Atlantis have once stood not too far from Fontaine Sallée in the French Languedoc?

Heracles tricked Atlas into holding aloft the Earth's sphere, and then left him there with nowhere to place his burden down again. This

Labour of Heracles seems to be situated in North Africa in today's Morocco, to south of the Pillars of Heracles. It was Heracles who brought the new tree-alphabet to Gades, Cadiz of today, from whence it reached Ireland where it was called the Boibel Loth. At Cadiz stood the Pillars of Heracles, four stone columns associated with the new calendar.

Atlas was twin-brother of Poseidon. Poseidon gave his brother land towards the Pillars of Heracles. Rennes le Châateau is no great distance from Cadiz. Poseidon built his Atlantis City, the land around being extremely fertile with an abundance of water, both hot and cold, the walls of his city being constructed of stones, white, red and black in colour. Take a look at the lands to the south of the Pillars of Heracles then make a choice between that and the Aude region of France.

Thera as Atlantis.

The most powerful of atomic-fusion weapons is a toy when compared with our planet's store of latent energy, that which is responsible for volcanic eruptions acting as a form of safety-valve.

Many a present-day volcano is much reduced in mass from that of a distant past.

During more recent times Krakatoa commenced to rumble prior to the first of a series of severe eruptions, some of which were literally felt in central Australia, and not as mere trembling of the ground.

Krakatoa is the main island of a group of three, the others being Lang and Verlaten islands. All three form a rough circle that lies between Java and Sumatra in the Indian Ocean to their west, the China Sea to east. As is the case with Aegean Thera, Krakatoa contains more than one volcanic cone.

For seven years Krakatoa gave advance warnings of what was to culminate in the greatest explosion of volcanic energy during modern times. On the 20th day of May, in the year 1883, fire eruptions commenced, their thunderous booms heard as far distant as one hundred miles.

Two days later, on May the 22nd the volcanoes' outpourings had reached upwards of seven miles into the atmosphere, dust falling 300 miles from the core.

It was not until August the 26/27th that Krakatoa literally exploded with unsurpassed fury, the estimated height reached by a massive cloud of steam and dust, above Krakatoa, being in the order of 15 miles.

With the coming of night, distant sailors observed fierce electrical activity in the cloud, equivalent of the ultimate in thunderstorms, whilst the volcano shone brightly. More explosions came, four in number and far more devastating than earlier ones. The dust-cloud now reached

50 miles, towering into a darkened sky, all lit by prolonged bursts of brilliant light, the noise reaching to deafening proportions.

Tidal waves commenced to form, a phenomenon to be expected when 5 cubic miles of volcanic material had been blown sky-high, some of it to fall down again creating ground-layers to depth of the equivalent of a twenty-storey building's height.

At 10:30am on the 26th a huge area remained black as night, the blasts breaking windows and walls fifty miles away. This was not the greatest of recorded, natural explosions of our era but it was the most violent, and felt all around the planet, tidal waves being immensely destructive, local villages and towns on coastal regions, inundated.

The noise was heard in Alice Springs, central Australia, 2200 miles in distance from the epi-centre. At approximately 55 miles from Krakatoa, at Telok Betong in Sumatra, flood-waves reached a height of 70 feet above normal sea-level. Here it was that a gunboat was carried inland, over a distance close to two miles, and left stranded at a height of 60 feet above sea-level. In open sea the waves reached an average height of 45 feet.

At that same time slight rises occurred in the waters of the English Channel, according to measuring devices both British and French.

Ships, as much as 3500 miles from Krakatoa, brought home faithful recordings, particularly of volcanic dust falling day after day onto the ocean surface, piling up over extensive areas to create islands of pumice as much as 2 feet in depth amid seas of thick mud. That is a lot of soot!

The aftermath of Krakatoa's Grand Exposition faded into history with brilliant sunsets seen across Europe and the North American continent.

The volcanic island of Thera can be measured against Krakatoa in the amount of energy released, effects and after-effects in like fashion now that professional archaeologists continue to explore islands of the Aegean which suffered from volcanic Thera's grand display of pyrotechnics some three-and-a-half millennia in the past. During this astounding eruption Thera lost more in surface-area than did the much later Krakatoa.

It is revealed that Thera disgorged dust over an area of 180,000 square miles. This eruption is also reputed to be the cause of decline in former Cretan sea-power, in mercantile and fighting ships. Anaphis island, no great distance from Thera, gives evidence of tidal waves that is assumed to reach 660 feet, or more than 66 storeys in height. It is accepted that Cretan palaces, built of brick and stone, and 100 miles from Thera, received severe damage to upper storeys.

From volcanic deposits archaeologists date the Thera eruptions from 1500 to 1470 BC, those deposits in the form of fine ash, being blown for hundreds of miles. There is a report of ships, at distant Alexandria, being carried above buildings in the harbour to be left on inner-city roads, so monumental were the tidal waves.

The deeper the water the faster that waves travel. Around Krakatoa the seas are up to 400 feet in depth. The sea, to the south of Thera, in which direction much of the explosive force travelled, reach depths more than six times that amount to give vastly-increased impetus to ensuing tidal-waves, and to their height.

Comparisons are made between the Thera eruption of 1500/1470 BC and that of 1650 AD, which latter generated far less natural power. Nevertheless the later eruption did produce tidal-waves reported as being 125 feet in height. From this eruption there resulted minor damage on Crete. So it comes as no surprise that the truly Big One brought about the collapse of a Minoan empire.

During construction of the Suez Canal a need for water-resistant mortar was a problem. Crushed pumice-stone, added to the mix, gave the desired effect. Upon the volcanic isle of Thera lay inexhaustible supplies of that material.

The Suez Canal Company removed enormous quantities of pumice at Akrotiri Bay on the southern coast of Thera. Whilst so-doing numerous stone blocks were exposed at lower, pumice levels. Further, now serious scientific excavations brought to light a multi-roomed habitation containing household goods that fleeing owners were unable to take with them. More walls, made of squared blocks, were found, standing surrounded by pumice, as were vaulted tombs of like antiquity.

Later finds included that which is entitled The House of Frescoes. It had that described as a rain-water cistern, a room of pitchers, frescoed walls, a roofed-over cellar, a staircase and skilfully-designed water conduit. The building was quite extensive, and typical of a Minoan construction. In shape and decorative style, the pitchers, or vases, were proven to be of Minoan origin.

In 1967 a Greek team of archaeologists set to work on Akritori. They unearthed intersecting walls. More pumice clearance revealed first a lamp with visible signs of soot upon it. Then came Minoan shards dating from shortly prior to the Great Eruption. A Minoan-type door-jamb was uncovered, later to be seen as a part of a window sill that gave access to a large room. Inside the room were six large, storage jars, some of them decorated in relief. Other finds suggested that the room served as a kitchen with hearth, beakers, a mortar and cooking-pot with tripod support among other ancient relics. All had been buried in a thick layer of pumice, including a cracked jar containing loom weights. The owners of the house had obviously escaped in desperate haste. Other remains indicated that upper storeys once existed at the spot. At another dig, evidence of a Minoan presence was further supported in the form of coloured wall-plaster.

For 2000 years the citizens of Crete formed the greatest power in the Aegean, with their ships voyaging in all directions to trade or colonize other lands and islands. They traded at Egyptian ports, and are known to have gone westward at least to Sicily.

There are those with fond memories of a once great British Empire which, in terms of years duration, was a mere shadow of the Minoan. From out of Crete came the first known great, naval power. With so much knowledge of the seas might Minoans have been among the Sons of Milen in Irish folklore? They did have all that was needed to travel even further than Malta and Sicily, as far as, or beyond, the Pillars of Heracles of later Grecian fame.

When giving his account of Atlantis Plato would most assuredly been familiar with the works of Herodotus who died only a few decades previously. Herodotus was aware that it was possible to circumnavigate the continent of Africa, a return journey made through the Red Sea, passing between the Pillars of Heracles on the outward-bound journey. He was also aware of a people to west of Egypt, living in the North African desert, people whom Herodotus call the Atlantes. They lived in the region containing Lake Tritonis, full of fresh water, which suddenly become saline due to the massive eruption of a volcano. Tidal waves, set in motion by Thera, provide the likeliest reason for the sea's inundation of the lake in northern Libya.

Pumice from Thera's eruption, fell over a huge area, much of it onto the waters of the Aegean Sea where it formed floating islands, and impassable mud as in Atlantis tradition. Land in the vicinity of volcanoes is prone to creation of springs of water, both hot and cold, to conform with those of Atlantis. Plato mentions use of stone in the colours white, red and black. These are the colours of the Triple Goddess, the same colour of stones Minoans used in their temples to their lunar-goddess. An island volcano with the familiar cone, with an outlying circular shoal of volcanic debris, the space between the two filled with sea-water, could well be described as having a circular canal.

The date of the Thera eruption gives a more reasonable time-span than does Plato's 9000 years.

Minoans were culturally far in advance of their Greek counterparts who were yet to become a nation.

Plato's Atlantis was excessively fertile.

The aptly-named Greenland, far to the north, is volcanic and highly fertile in its soil, warmth from the Earth's core making possible the production of crops. Thera, at the Mediterranean latitude, must have been a virtual paradise on Earth, warmer in winter than on non-volcanic islands, it's pumiced soil highly fertile, sufficiently so for production of those luxurious crops that Egyptians craved and bought. Fertile Atlantis could not have done better.

Solon's Egyptian priest spoke of Athenians overcoming the armies of Atlantis. If one thinks in terms of Mycenaens under a Greek veil, Mycenaeans who replaced greatly weakened Minoans as the dominant force in the eastern Mediterranean, the priest's story becomes acceptable.

Take away Plato's narrator's highly-glossed embroideries and Thera fits the Atlantis theme better than any other place on Earth. Or does it?

Of Gods not Men

Not again! Yes! Following upon the uncertain footsteps of Erik von Daniken gods were once upon Earth to control the destinies of humankind. 'We shall build you pyramids for your sons to marvel upon, and the sons of your sons unto the Nth. generation. Not that they shall serve a useful service, those pyramids, for your sons must toil for the planting of crops, and later harvesting of that same, in order that they shall live.'

According to one Allan Alford, author of Gods of the New Millennia, questioning the earlier work of Zecharia Sitchin, as to the chronology of events, biblical or otherwise, is in competition with Sitchin who, for instance, places the birth of Adam at 2123 BC with the Flood at 2415 BC according to his terms of reference.

Alford employs his particular version of the Sumerian king-lists in pursuit of his own theories, gods and all that this implies. He tells of a star called Nibiru, the cycle of which is a precise 3600 years- solar and in conjunction with the precessional cycle of 25920 years, yet one more precise figure in which Aquarius moves through it's celestial path to return to it's former position among the stars. Round figures do make easier the resolving of calculations. Alford next goes to some length to equate 3600 with 2160 years.
$$25920 \div 12 = 2160.$$
We read that Nibiru, star, or planet in this context, has an eliptical orbit. So Alford's SAR becomes 2160 Earth-years.

So the gods arrive ,as it seems inevitable they must,in Alford's SARS at 270183 BC, whereas Sitchin's arrive at 443000 BC, which latter is much nearer to the figures in my particular Sumerian King-lists, that of 456,000 Earth-years.

We have gods on Earth at 270183 BC.
gods in rebellion-183783 BC.
The Flood-10983 BC, according to Alford.

Somewhere, in all of this, busy-body Thoth appears who, following his construction of Stonehenge, flew across the Atlantic Ocean to organize the building of Mayan pyramids and to dabble about with the Mayan calendar.

Swift as lightning Thoth then nips across to China (To build the Great Wall?) then back to Bahrain upon the Persian Gulf, to construct an observatory. Since the given date, for the arrival of Thoth in Mexico, is 2900 BC, he had little time to organize and instruct the labour-force at Stonehenge.

Later, Alford tells of a Garden of Eden, and naturally includes Eve born, shall you believe it, 176,583 BC. Indeed a goddess of renown! But, in name, EVE is derived from Hebrew HIWWA, in turn rooted in HERWA, foremost goddess of the Hittites.

We also learn of third-century BC Berossus, both priest and historian who, wishing to impress his knowledge upon Greek historians, Apollondorus among them, told of ten Chaldean kings whose collective reigns span 432,000 Earth-years. But 432,000 is a figure to be found in the Vishnu Epic. At the time of Berossus, and earlier, it was common for historians to travel far in search of information relating to events of the past. I propose that in this manner did Berossus gain his information.

Alford supplies a list of eight Sumerian kings' lengths of reign. In Earth-years they comprise 8-10-12-8-10-14 and 5 SARS, which total, when multiplied by his 2160, does not comply with my Sumerian source by a large margin.

67 x 2160 = 144,720, whereas I have 456,000 in solar years.

I place more faith in figures reached by archaeological interpretation of tablets of clay, representing the Sumerian King- lists than I do in the figures this self-appointed historian, Alford who does submit that the priestly-historian's figures must come from another geographical location than that of Babylon. Well, Chaldea is Babylon of today's Iraq, and ancient Sumeria

The Vishnu Epic 432,000, shared with that of Berossus, does contain some direct parallels with calculations based upon my version of the Sumerian King-lists. There is nothing of the mystery in any of the Sumerian, Vishnu and Babylonian figures, except for the fact they were formulated at so early a date. And the author's birth of the Sumerian Culture is supposed to pre-date the Flood by an extra-ordinary number of years. Since I have mathematical proof that Stonehenge pre-dates Sumer, then Stonehenge, too was constructed before Alford's date for the Flood, this in defiance of modern techniques by which the first stage of Stonehenge would be only a few years earlier than 3000BC.

Multiply Sitchin's SAR of 3600 by 10, answer 36000. The dimensions of Solomon's temple are 60 x 30 x 20 equalling 36000. This is a figure to be found in my version of the King-lists.

I made further enquiries, from an official source, in order to confirm the date for my particular king-lists. I was informed that they date back to 2500 BC. If one accepts 2500 BC how many centuries of observation of lunar cycles preceded this? They, therefore, pre-date Berossus by a couple of millennia, he obtaining ready-made information at that.

The word KING, where applied in this context, is misleading, as is any substitution of GODS.

Of Gods that Never Were

I compliment those authors for their diligence but not their theories in which the evolution of humankind is assisted by gods, and, super-humans of greatly-advanced knowledge and techniques. Eric von Daniken has his intellectual disciples of today, even though less flamboyant in presentation of their material. They serve only to detract from the intelligence and abilities of our distant forebears.

I have no scientific background, I who prefer the fundamental approach to any ancient mystery awaiting answers, and become automatically-with good reason-suspicious of any claims that humankind cannot, unaided by super-beings, have constructed Stonehenge nor the pyramids of Egypt and Mexico. In terms of mathematical calculation I have the key in such as the Vishnu Epic of India, the Sumerian King-lists, and to Stonehenge, which proves that all three share something in common. I do not suggest that people from any of the countries involved ever met face to face. Nor do I suggest that super-humans transmitted the requisite knowledge from country to country.

Throughout the Ancient world religious hierarchies, steeped in The Mysteries, held power over their superstitious followers by down-right trickery. Moses employed trickery to turn a serpent into a staff. He, trained by an Egyptian priesthood, struck a rock with his staff to produce water in the desert, an example of prior knowledge of a natural phenomenon, the secret of which is known only to members of the priesthood.

A volcano explodes with tremendous power; a pillar of dark ash is thrown many kilometres into the atmosphere. Lightening is seen to play inside that column spreading in all directions overhead. The sun is blacked out, night and day indistinguishable one from another. So the sun stood still according to legend. The gods were indeed angered!

Respected scholars accept that worship of the Mother Goddess preceded that of gods. Beneath much window dressing this is what the Creation theme is describing, a transition from a goddess-worshiping matriarchal society to that of the patriarchal. In spite of Moses' autocratic God, the Hebrews continued to worship in High Places, at their temples to the Goddess.

There are two Creation stories in the Bible, the first of them given a few brief words, the Elohim Creation. As Robert Graves informs us, Astarte was a member of the Elohim. And what of the Biblical Lilith? Men of the Church avoid mention of this goddess who sent handmaidens to assist Yahweh with that particular Creation.

Apparently it is possible to produce others, but the earlier Sumerian King- lists cover a period of 456,000 years in human terms. Are we to assume that the reigns of these kings commenced so far back in time? The Vishnu Epic comprises an overall equivalent of 4 x 432,000 years-human. Surely those kings were indeed gods. How else explain their longevity? I admit that the Epic concerns gods. But they are allegorical.

Deities, of whichever gender, will have been with us since humans gained self-awareness, to look in wonder at all around them, marvelling at much that we, scientifically-conditioned, take as normal. Their's was the Age of magic and miracles, requiring an indefinable something, a spiritual prime-driver to explain why day or night, hot or cold, wet or dry, calm or tempest, life, birth and death. And the foods that they found free for the taking from bough and briar, and from both above and below the earth, fish in the waters, and beasts for the killing.

They knew when the Goddess was angry, great storms heralding her wrath.. They knew then the Goddess was tranquil, all of Nature at peace.

Cycles of time would be recognized, in seasons, in sky-bodies, in life-spans, birth and death. Females would become aware of personal cycles, which had a strange association with the moon.

We know from archaeological discoveries that they revered their dead, graves-goods indicating that they believed in a life hereafter, as did Egyptian pharaohs, much later.

We evolve as intended by Nature, probably now in the final stage, for Nature appears to possess a built-in regulator which keep any particular section of the animal species at a manageable level. The human race has grown to big for it's Raebocks, has it not?

Darwin's great theory is attacked, and rightly so. But his natural selection does require time to work. It has all the time in the world -a small slice from the Universe- in this to progress from original state to final image. Man, and Woman-where-would-we-be-without-her, of course, must have evolved in a series of mutations, it is claimed in order to explain apparent leaps in human intelligence during the six million years of human evolution. The mutationists consider that to be insufficient a time for us to have reached our present form without outside aid.

Animals do it: humans do it, from a sense of need. That is to say that they overcome a problem out of a need to do so. It is that need which is responsible for developement of the brain coupled with some degree of instinct.

In his 'Gods of the new Millennium' Alan Alford places much faith in his type of gods to define how great achievements of our distant ancestors were wrought, his gods at work, not human beings. Such an insistence insults our forebears, in their being incapable of feats of technological expertize of any type.

Mankinds' earliest tools were crude lumps of stone used for such tasks as smashing bone to get to the marrow, for instance. A length of stick might serve a variety of purposes. Throughout hundreds of thousands of years improvement was slow. Then they learnt how to make use of flint. Much depended what type of raw material was available. Well before the advent of a Sumerian civilization boats were used, in the Aegean to transport obsidian, a black volcanic glass, long distances from the volcanic region of, to that which became mainland Greece. Such a glass could be employed as a mirror, chipped into razor-sharp slivers for delicate cutting operations.

Where invention and relatively-swift advances to improvement in the necessities of life are concerned, Alan Alford and company might spend some hours examining the artifacts on show at the Musée de Pré-histoire at Les Eyzies, Dordogne, France. Here, during the last ice-age, Cro-Magnon Man replaced the Neanderthal. The flints on display range from the cruder to the extremely refined, from larger tools in stone to the extremely delicate and slender flakes, of which were special-purpose blades requiring a dainty touch in the cutting. These Cro-Magnons wore well-cut clothing, coats with toggle fasteners, and trousers, button-holed and stitched. They wore hats and shoes, that your man or woman about the village must flaunt.

These most inventive of people cut themselves arrow and spear-heads, unlike previous examples off which the prey may well slide, with barbs, even multi-barbed, shaped with care, to maintain a beautiful balance. Their hardwood needles are the equal, in every respect, to the modern needle in steel, from the very small to the large in size.

They invented a contraption that became an extension of the throwing-arm to give extra propulsion to their spears. They had bows and arrows too, weapons developed for the killing of a prey from longer distances. Safer for the hunter. Even weapons embodied an elegance to be found in most other of their artifacts.

These, once classed as no more than wild beasts, by the Church in particular, with it's dogma of the Creation, people who wove cloth from the wool of sheep, flax and hemp. They had lamps, fire, stout shelters and retired to the depths of caves only when it became too cold to live in open air. Cro-Magnon Man had a height of 1.8 metres, about 6 feet. They are from the late Paleolithic era, comprising the

Aurignacien, Solutrien, Mesolithic periods followed by the Mesolithic era broken down into the Azilian, Tardeoisien, and Sauveterrien. Next comes the Neolithic Campignien and Robenhausen, named after French localities of associated archaeological excavation, with the exception of the last-named, which is Swiss. This, as a whole, covers a period of some 40,000-years duration during which relatively-short time human-beings advanced from a brutish way of life to an organized and highly-creative mode of existence. This required an increase in power of the brain, the right hemisphere's functions increasing in variety whilst those of the left hemisphere deteriorated, with less use of the wits and instincts needed for survival in a hostile environment. The Neolithic, of course, brought the use of metals.

In long periods of time, stage by stage in terms of inventiveness, advancements in technology have accelerated, a capacity for intellectual progress, essential for this, also accelerating. Following hundreds of thousands of years with crude forms of tools came the mere 40,000 years of refinement and progress, as is to be seen at the Les Eyzies Museum to Pre-history. By comparison progress from tools of beaten copper to the sophistication of today's machines and computers spans a mere four to five thousand years.

In only eighty years war has left the trenches to become that which we now observe. And now mankind is probing the stars, not one of Alan Alford's gods indicating their presence, no sign of Mutationist progress in the brain of modern man.

In all of the above rests an anomaly which is beyond me to resolve. In cubic capacity the brain of Cro-Magnon Man was considerably greater than that of his modern counterpart. Does Alford's mutation-theory work in reverse? Is it possible that from the earliest days of employment of artificial means of calculation, the human brain becomes smaller through the lack of intense concentration once required of it?

Unlike our ancient forebears we live in conditioned environments, largely protected from the less welcome vicissitudes of Nature. We no longer have need of those senses that were essential for survival by Early Man, whose sense of smell, hearing and eyesight assisted in forewarning of approaching danger. A lack of necessity, in those senses, means a reduction in their acuteness for we of today. The part of the brain that no longer serves its former function will wither away. So much for advances in computer science!

So there went the more-visible trait in Man, Woman, too, of course.

They once had need of it to protect themselves from the weather, and the heat of the sun, their body-hair. With artificial modes of guarding the flesh hair became redundant. One does see, upon occasion, a throw-back to an earlier era, some bare-chested fellow with an expanse of coconut matting across his upper torso, a Neanderthal throw-back. Thank goodness that the sun-worshipping girls of Mimizan la Plage (upon the Atlantic coast to south of Bordeaux) do not show signs of being descended from the Neanderthal types. Ladies of the night-hours? They are those with the paler flesh.

From whence came the Tuatha de Danaan?

Far more recently my interest in our pre-historic past led me into the selection of a library-book, entitled The Megaltihic Odyssey, author Christian O'Brien. When making my choice I failed to note that, apart from much intelligent research into megalithic sites on Bodmin Moor the book contained more than a mention of the Tuatha de Danaan, alternatively spelt Danann.

I recalled that Robert Graves, in his The White Goddess, traced the Tuatha de Danaan back to the vicinity of the Dardanelles and Black Sea. Christian O'Brien takes them even further back in time and place, to the Anannage of ancient Sumeria.

Leaving aside modern New-towns and the like, place-names invariably reveal some aspect of topographical features close to where the village or town is placed, the name itself having gone through a series of modifications in spelling throughout centuries.

Archaeological interpretations of evidence, recorded long ago, rely heavily upon the use of etymology. Christian O'Brien spent years in lands bordering the Persian Gulf during which time he acquired a strong feel for the region's historic past. Such a close affinity with the area enabled the author to produce an exciting hypothesis based upon extensive research into the pasts of ancient races of peoples who suddenly, and inexplicably, burgeon from a primitive state of existence to that of civilized nations.

In the sagas of people, as diverse as Scandinavia to Central America in origin, one is all too frequently confronted with mention of sages, persons of vastly superior knowledge and abilities, who may also be described as teachers, with god-like auras, and who become the goddesses and gods of folklore. They teach wild savages how to till the soil, plant the seed and irrigate the crops, organize the workforce, and reveal how to measure time by observations made of cycles to be found in stars, sun and moon. To the Celts, Druids were sages.

To uncultured herders of goats and sheep, to primitive farmers and hunters, who had time only for concentration upon day to day tasks with no thought for the future, learn-ed sages would appear to have been sent by the gods, if not the gods themselves come to improve the lot of people on Earth. Those same sages would not divulge all of their secrets, thereby retaining sufficient a halo of mystique which placed them firmly established as workers of the miraculous who could predict the coming of awesome eclipses of moon and sun, the rising of certain stars or groups of. Such prophets could not be human.

By the introduction of systematic farming, of organized irrigation and fertilization of crops they would give practical demonstrations of how brilliant they were to lowly farmers who formerly tilled the land to exhaustion without putting anything back in order to retain the soil's richness. Now, the farmer would no longer be forced to move on every few years in search of fresh pastures, or starve. Only the gods could achieve such super human miracles.

I am forced to associate those sages with the Mystery Schools from Egypt and Hellenic Greece, in which the secrets of vine-grafting, the times to plough, sow and harvest, the turning of grain to flour and the grape into wine, were closely-guarded against revelation to the provincial. O'Brien informs us that the sages appeared apparently out of nowhere, of antecedents they have none. It was they who were responsible for the creation of gigantic earthworks and megalithic structures in stone, such as are to be detected in Ireland and mainland Britain. He accepts the more likely interpretation of Tuatha de Danaan as being Tribe of the Goddess Danae, or Danann and, as does Graves, informs us that the Danes, whose country is Denmark, owe the origins of the generic name to the Tuatha who brought Goddess Danae with them when reaching that land.

O'Brien describes how, in accordance with Irish legend, there are three gods of the Tuatha de Danaan, one for each order of newcomers, those of leaders, scientists and crafts-persons, extraordinary beings with skills that only magicians possessed.

Ancient records, like those impressed into the cuneiform tablets of early Sumerians, supported by oral traditions, enable researchers to trace Neolithic peoples from when they first appear in history to their later movements and influences in territories that they reach. When writing of numerical correspondences to be noted in the Sumerian King-lists and Stonehenge circles I purposely disassociated one people from the other, suggesting no physical contact between them. I now read the work of O'Brien and am forced to re-appraise the situation. Parties can be seen linked by dissemination of knowledge through the auspices of those called the Anannage.

O'Brien brings attention to simultaneous events taking place during early centuries of the third millennium BC. They range from construction of Mesopotamian ziggurats, early Egyptian pyramids to huge earthworks as far afield as Britain and Ireland. The author asks did those responsible share a common heritage?

To pre-Hellenic Greeks the Minoans would been seen as a super-race, not so much for their powerful armies and navies but primarily because of their cultural knowledge and refined arts, the Favoured of the Gods. Perhaps Favoured of the Goddess would be more apt for evidence points to a former sacrificing of Minoan kings to the Goddess whilst deities of early Cretan origin are decidedly of the female gender to be given new names and be demoted by invading Greeks.

O'Brien tells of the Anannage whose arrival, to the east of Lebanon and Syria, brought about a cultural revolution to the region around 2500BC. These Anannage, according to translation of Sumerian cuneiform tablets, are referred to as Lords, the Heavenly Assembly, the Great Sons of Anu, the Wise Ones, gods in other words. Whatever, and wherever, the epithet applied it is always highly complimentary to the Anannage.

The Sumerian Anu is to be equated with legendary Anu of Ireland where the goddess is also to be found in names such as AN, Ainne and Aine.

The Tuatha de Danaan are directly associated with the building of pre-historic erections at Irish Knowth, New Grange and Dowth. There is the Mound of Anu (Cnoc Ainne) and the Two Paps of Anu (Da Chich Danainne) among other notable names. Some of Ireland's pagan deities live on in Christian guise as saints, the foremost among them Anu who becomes St. Anne, with Bridget in like manner becoming St. Bride.

The Tuatha de Danaan, Mother of all Gods, is modified to Dana, also spelt Danu meaning, as with the epithets Anu, Aine and Ainne, Bright or Radiant.

As place-names change in letter-form, in the passage of time, so do characters in folklore whilst retaining some major aspect of the original. Celtic Saeferne became our Severn, the river of that name. Avon would have been Aeferne. with *Laeferne* Brook.

Movement of the Tuatha is traced from the Middle East, across Europe through Denmark, Scandinavia, France and Mainland Britain to Scotland from whence they crossed over to Ireland, where legend says that they first burnt their boats prior to concealing themselves within a magical mist that concealed them from local inhabitants during a three-day march inland. It is significant that they arrived at Beltaine, a pagan sun-festival which, according to a solar calendar, would be May the 11/12th, Gregorian, a time for the performance of High Magic. Those same people disappear as mysteriously as they arrived to become the elves and fairies of Irish folklore.

Who taught the Sumerians the various arts attributed to them? It is known that farming and the art of smelting gold and silver employing the lost-wax principal to form decorative artifacts, existed before their time. The easy answer to the question may never be forthcoming unless it rests within that over-fertile mind of Eric von Daniken.

Intruding into Sumerian records are words from an entirely different source. It was these anomalies that gave Christian O'Brien the clue he sought. He admits that he was not the first to question their appearance.

The river-names Tigris and Euphrates are not Sumerian just as some local place-names of importance are not. Among other non-Sumerian words are those applicable to agriculture, metalworkers, carpenters, potters, masons, weavers, leatherworkers, smiths and merchants, all of them a necessary part in the civilizing of a people, the very backbone of an organized society. Once these skills were established a nation would be ready for further advancement in other spheres of endeavour.

O'Brien reasons that such skills and crafts were introduced by teachers, the Anannage sages.

It was, according to Sumerian texts, the gods who taught them how to construct houses of wood, who showed them the way to organized planting of grain, control of water channeled through systems of irrigation, all instruction given in the language of the Anannage whom Sumerians call The Bright Ones, the Gods, when still living in a primitive state. It is here that we come across the non-Sumerian word, AN, meaning Heaven, or Pnu, the Highly Revered, extended to Great Sons of Anu, Great Sons of Heaven, et cetera. These accolades run parallel with those directed at Ireland's Tuatha de Danaan, even to use of the names An and Mu.

The Anannage Bright Ones overlord city states, of their own creation, in Sumeria for many centuries before suddenly vanishing as completely as did the Tuatha de Danaan from Ireland. The Sumerians' teachers disappeared sometime during the later stages of the third millennium BC.

The author progresses step by step in an etymological analysis of words in which lie elements common to a number of ancient tongues whilst seeking further evidence supportive of his Anannage hypothesis, no possible path overlooked, of which latter was the apocryphal Secrets of Enoch.

Enoch speaks of Angel-watchers on Mount Hermon who proceed to teach mankind of things of great value, of how to farm the land, work with metals, weather-lore and an understanding of solar and lunar signs, which last I interpret as being their cycles. Dubbed angels and archangels these sages have strong correlations with the Anannage of Sumeria.

A reference to Osiris is also worthy of study, the Egyptian god who taught the savages, along the Nile, how to make agricultural instruments, plant the vine and the grain, the making of bread, wine and beer, arts that the Anannage introduced in Sumeria and elsewhere.

Osiris, having civilized Egypt, is recorded as having a desire to spread his knowledge elsewhere throughout the World.

There is nothing mystical about the Secrets of Enoch when one translates his words in terms of superior mortals who descend upon barbaric people with no planned economies, to raise them from the precarious life of nomads to settled and profitable levels, with a form of government to oversee agriculture and industry upon a planned basis. For angels read Anannage. Enoch's archangels, Gabriel and company, are Anannage lords. And indeed of human guise.

The Anannage decide that the time has arrived for their civilization of peoples to north and west of the Mediterranean Sea. They journey across the Dardenelle strait into Greece, perhaps en route giving the people of Crete their blessing. Somewhere along the way they become the Tuatha de Danaan, wherever they travel finding time to erect their megalithic trademarks in stone, as did later Mycenaeans in the very same areas. They had need of their stone circles and outlying cairns or solitary menhirs in order to observe movements of stars, moon and sun, Stonehenge probably their greatest observatory of all.

O'Brien, once again delving into etymology, suggests that Danann (a form of Danaan) is an expansion of De and Anann which is more than an indicator of an Anannage influence. I here reproduce an extract from The Megalithic Odyessy.... *After this the sixth place, and there I saw seven groups of Angels, very bright and wonderful, with faces shining brighter than the Sun. They were brilliant and all dressed alike and looked alike. Some of these Angels study the movements of the Stars, the Sun and Moon, and record the peaceful order of the World. Other Angels there, undertake teaching and give instructions in clear, melodious voices. These are the Archangels who are promoted over ordinary Angels. They are responsible for recording and studying the fauna and flora in both the highlands and the lowlands.*

There are Angels who record the seasons and years; others who study the rivers and seas; others who study the fruits of the lowlands, and the plants and herbs which give nourishment to the animal kingdom. And, there, Angels study Mankind and record the behaviour of men, and how they live.

When one is confronted with the image of angels, as described by Enoch, beings who dictate their superior knowledge to ordinary humans, and mix with them, on a face to face basis, in order to see their instructions carried out in the correct manner, is it any wonder that the Church omits such fraternizing from it's teachings? And why should supposedly heavenly angels have need to study such mundane factors on Earth?

The foregoing few pages are insufficient in a delivery of the full impact of Christian O'Brien's masterly investigation into the ancient world of teachers and sages, his transformation of former gods to earthly human beings who, as wonder-workers of the miraculous, become deified by those whom they guide and instruct. The author's hypothesis is well-worth the reading in full.

An Archaeological Conumdrum.

Throughout my research I am forced to rely upon the historic-dating of experts, not all necessarily in full agreement one with another.

Reference is sometimes made to a Greek Dark Age, a period of 500 years during which the Mycenaean civilization appeared to abruptly vanish only to reappear, with equal suddenness, five centuries on, this the archaeological view. Yet their evidence is more than somewhat confusing.

If the theory is correct then Mycenaean artisans, and their products, vanished to leave no trace of their labours, from that time forward. What might have caused so great a calamity?

The Victorian era gave rise to men intelligent and rich enough to venture forth in search of hidden history, this by exploration of Near Eastern lands, adventurers with tents, picks and shovels, earnest men who would later write books upon their discoveries, their chosen discipline in its infancy. Some selected to go to the former Mycenae.

When a Temple to Hera was excavated it was finally dated 1300 to 1200 BC, this in accordance with the age of pottery uncovered at the site. This gave rise to much learned discussion, and controversy, because, intermingled with that early pottery was more which, when compared with pottery elsewhere, was from the 8-7th. BC.

Mycenaean pottery was used to date the famous Lion Gate. 8th. century they exclaimed. A later trench was dug in an effort to discover why the sudden demise of all things Mycenaean, in terms of 1100 BC,.they found nothing to indicate why. Yet that later bunch of glory-seekers found pottery, in their trench, a mixture of both 12th and 7th century ware.

Of course, once a dating-system has been established, and accepted as a *fait accompli* by learned men, it will never be shaken until a new process of dating arrives by which means correction can be made. And then with reluctance from the Old Brigade, authors of tomes in need of modification.

So what do decorative tiles, from the reign of Ramesses 111 prove? Upon their reverse sides are letters from the Greek alphabet, an alphabet awaiting a further 400 years or so, for it's invention, if the dating system is reliable. Doubtless, that alphabet was compiled long before it was employed at a commercial level, its letters upon the backs of tiles, denoting who made them perhaps, as well as showing a Greek origin for them.

Homer was thought to have compiled some attractive works of fiction, this to be disproved when a number of cities, mentioned by the poet, were disinterred with their various levels of destruction and re-erection at that site.

Greeks considered their poet to have written of the Trojan war within a generation of the event. This brings that war forward, from 1250 BC to circa 750 BC. I accept the Greek opinion.

However, that old fixation with a Greek Dark Age had its effect with contemporaneous excavations in bordering lands, where the dating-system was based upon that of Mycenae. In spite of conflicting evidence many, of today, insist upon giving the war with Troy a 1250 BC date.

First Age of the Aude. Pre-historic.

Exploration of Landscape.

The technology of land surveying along geometric lines, is fairly ancient in origin. Greeks, of the era that brought Aristotle into prominence, possessed quite refined instruments for carrying out such a task, graduated and superior to the later Roman device of that nature.

When in the Holy Land, Knights Templar learnt much that was unavailable in Western Europe, from Arab populations, the use of refined herbal remedies. Advanced mathematics, astronomy, existence of the magnetic compass and fairly accurate land survey by which to create useful maps of immediate localities to be included.

With whom the discovery, that I am about to describe, originated, lacking archaeological evidence, I have been unable to establish. Nevertheless, I favour a Greek hand in it. Greek adventurers, such as those who were to colonize some coastal areas of Southern France, as well as travel inland to the Atlantic coast en route to Cornwall, with its sources for tin and copper. Any triangle, with sides in proportions of 3:4:5, must contain a right-angle. I state the obvious in that each of the four corners, of a rectangle contain angles of 90°s of arc.

When one has a great variety of landscape features, upon which to draw, such as those to be found in the southern aspects of my map of the Aude Département of the Languedoc-Roussillon region of France, ancient churches, châteaux, fortress-ruins, grottoes, old mine-workings, single tombs, cemeteries and the like, one is in a position to create alignments, Ley-line in style, a mixture of elements of differing dates and origins with over-enthusiastic eagerness. British Ley-lines are of this nature more often than not, some of the controlling-features difficult to miss, so great the area that they cover, therefore suspect. Hill-forts can cover several acres.

Although it is possible that people superimposed their own sacred sites upon those of earlier inhabitants, thus making acceptable the employment of such sites for purposes of alignment searches, either for one era or another but generally not both together. Examples of such dual purpose sites are to be seen today in Christian cathedrals and churches which were deliberately constructed by papal decree, at former sites for worship by pagans. Throughout the task I remained alert to alignments with possible bearing upon solstice positions, this without success until late into my quest. My alignments must be controlled by all-enduring stone in one or other form.

Our ancient forebears, lacking artificial means to record time, showed great interest in the sun's position upon horizons, especially at the equinoxes and solstices which provide natural divisions for the year. Whilst giving my map concentrated attention, in the area of the French Aude region, to east of Quillan, I kept that in mind.

The Rennes les Bains' latitude is at 42°55', whereas, for the year 2000, our era, the summer-solstice azimuth is 56.17°s, and for the year 2000 BC, it would be 55.38°s as fractions of a degree, a difference of less than one degree of arc yet, small though that appears to be, still huge in terms of astronomy.

I prepared to commence with a clean slate, so-to-say, in execution of my map-survey whilst purposely avoiding any mixture in points of reference.

My original map, purchased from Blackwell's of Oxford, was of a 1:25,000 scale, roughly 1800 x 1600 millimetres, or 6 x 4 feet in size.

My insistence upon stone alone possessed another merit for, unlike wooden posts, it will not decay.

I set the map flat upon a sheet of hardboard with A2 sheets of clear acetate to give protection to it during operations. My pens were of the finest-points for mapping routines, a spool of thinnest black thread among my remaining needs. One should keep in mind how those ancient of our forebears, when constructing passage-graves, were able to move pieces of rock of phenomenal weight and size.

I examined the map, seeking a suitable point at which to begin. Pech de Bugarach, with its 1230 metres above sea-level, triangulation-point, might well provide the best place, as a controlling element that some pre-historic new arrival may well select for visual surveys of the locality.

Go to any place of choice, at one or other of the equinoxes, and you will find that the sun rises due to east with sunset due to west. This fact suggested that I place my first horizontal line, inked in upon the sheet of acetate-film, to run west to east through the peak's 1230 M triangulation-point.

Some experimentation followed, curiosity deciding that I place in a vertical line from the church at Rennes le Château, one that cut the Pech de Bugarach west-east line to south. For me this became quite acceptable because that tiny village, perched high above surrounding land, at 500M, asl.(above sea-level). had once been home to a pre-Christian temple, to Isis according to some historian. It matters not which the goddess: that it was of so early a date was suited to the time which the local dolmen indicated by its position, within the final arrangement of pre-historic alignments, confirming its validity. I entered a line going to east from the Rennes le Château church, where it met a second vertical that arose from the Pech de Bugarach point. I now had four alignments enclosing a perfect rectangle. I placed in the diagonals.

The map-reproduction is taken from a French Béziers/Perpignan IGN TOP 100, 174 map, scale 1:100,000, the lined box of a scale reduced in size from my original set upon a French Series Bleue map 2347 OT, TOP 25, Quillan/Alet-les-Bains 1:25,000 scale, its topographical features, both pre-historic and present era, far greater in number, therefore all the better arranged for any potential Ley-hunter's benefit. In this case I purchased a second 1:25,000 scale map that adjoins the eastern side of the former, to include Camp-sur-Agly with its nearby and important dolmen and cairns, a 2447 OT, TOP 25, Tuchan Series Bleue.

Incidentally, relative to Plato's Atlantis stones in white, red and black, which will later arise, sources for these can be detected upon the Quillan/Alets-les-Bains map.

An Exploration Continued.

I had my rectangle controlled by the Pech de Bugarach height, and time to set about some careful measurements as accurate as a 1:25,000 map permits.

I checked and re-checked. I stretched a length of finest thread from point to point, and repeated the task, suspicious as I was of such precise figures. The thread was as fine as a human hair of a blonde type, perhaps in the order of one-tenth of one-millimetre in thickness.

With the rectangle's diagonals in place I had three dimensions from which to check linear proportions in that design.

The rectangle's short side gave 28.5cms, the long side 38.0cms.
With diagonals that gave 47.5cms.
$$28.5 \div 3 = 9.5 \text{cms.}$$
$$38.0 \div 4 = 9.5 \text{cms.}$$
$$47.5 \div 5 = 9.5 \text{cms.}$$
Here was confirmation that all linear aspects of the rectangle were in proportions of 3:4:5. I continued to find difficulty in accepting the truth of my discovery.

I have given angular values, in degrees of arc, for the following two geometric diagrams observed upon a map of the French Aude/Languedoc-Roussillon Département, numerical designations as listed below.

90°s (of arc)
$$57+°\text{s.}$$
$$53+°\text{s}$$
$$37-°\text{s of arc.}$$
Basic mathematics do not lie but they can be manipulated to serve some pre-meditated concept which they hope will not receive close examination.

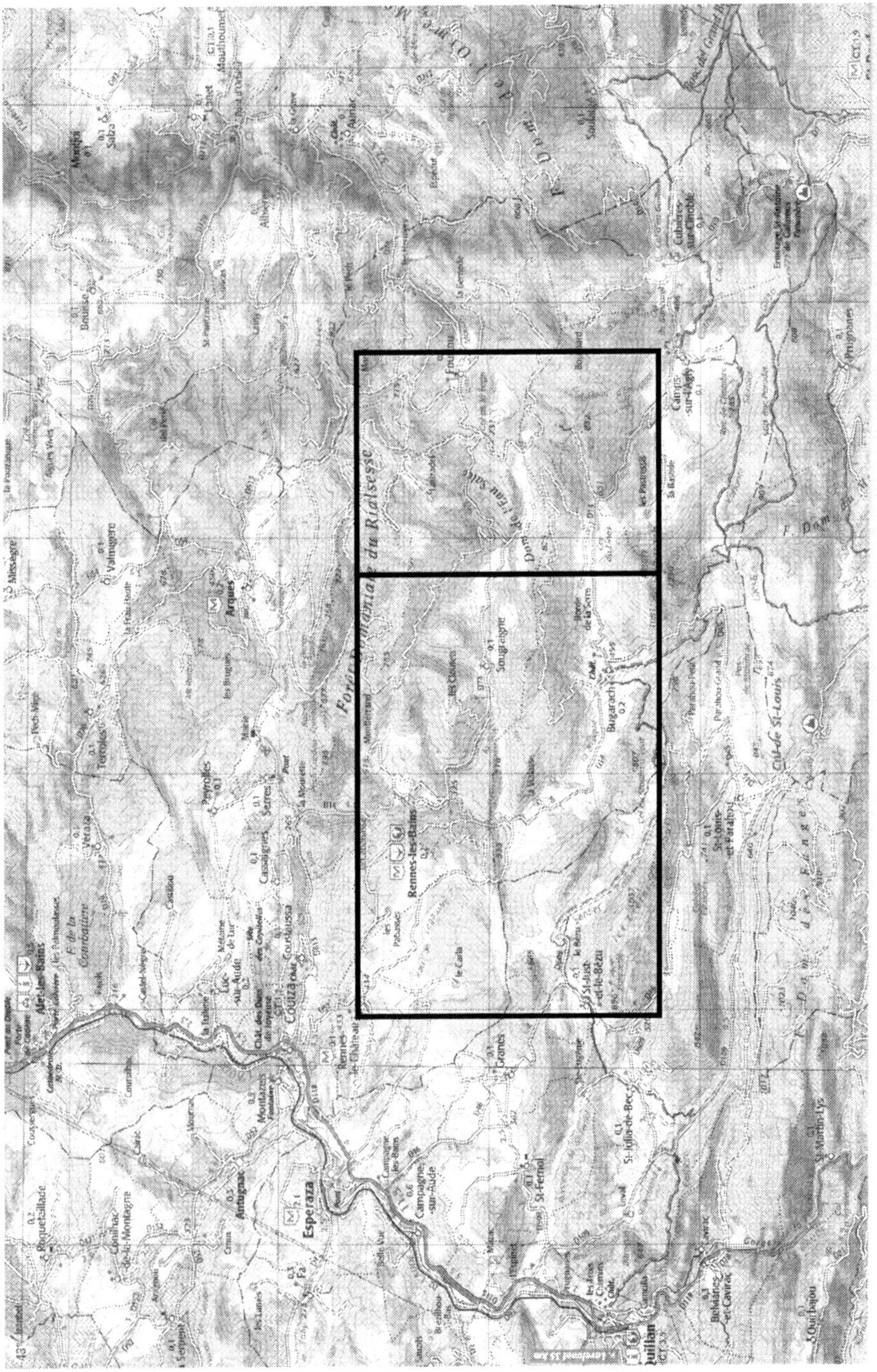
Rennes-les-Bains
Bugarach
Esperaza
Arques
Sougraigne
Campagne-sur-Aude
St-Ferriol
Cubières-sur-Cinoble
Col-de-St-Louis
Quillan
Serres
Peyrolles
Alet-les-Bains
Missègre
Valmigère
Terroles
Antugnac
St-Julia-de-Bec
St-Just-et-le-Bézu
Granès

In anticipation of a question that may arise, I am unable to provide any firm answer as to how this landscape geometry was originally formed.

Within the bounds of the rectangle, the diagonals make up four triangles in number.

I had no more, no less than a bare-boned diagram, a rectangle whose size was controlled by only two landscape features, those of Pech de Bugarach and the Rennes le Château church, the latter, admittedly, assumed to be built over a known pagan site from antiquity, that would have been some type of temple erected to a goddess, perhaps to include a statue to the lady.

I continued to feel a little dubious about that round-figure 38 cms. dimension, with the other two to only one-place of decimal, their 0.5 terminations. Nonetheless, there existed an element which suggested, to me, that I had little to lose in progressing further by following up even the slightest of possible clues. It was later that I travelled to Blackwell's of Oxford, specializing in maps, from whom to purchase a replacement map, ordered in advance, of the same area of the French Languedoc-Roussillon.

Here is a word of warning!

With care I put the new map in position, took the sheet of clear acetate, upon which I had penned the rectangle from the first map, and placed it to cover the same area as upon the old map. I saw a discrepancy; the penned rectangle failed to fit the new map as precisely as hoped. The error was approximately by one millimetre. Such disappointment!

Not to be down-hearted without checking the error in more than one direction, I took a metricated straight-edge, then measured and checked distances for corresponding equivalents of 20 kilometres upon the ground, this both vertically and horizontally. Both measurements, from the old map, were of the

The Pech de Bugarach/ Rennes-le Chateau Rectangle, plus it's Extension.
This diagram is not to scale. Numerous triangles with 3,4,5 proportioned sides can be developed from this base.

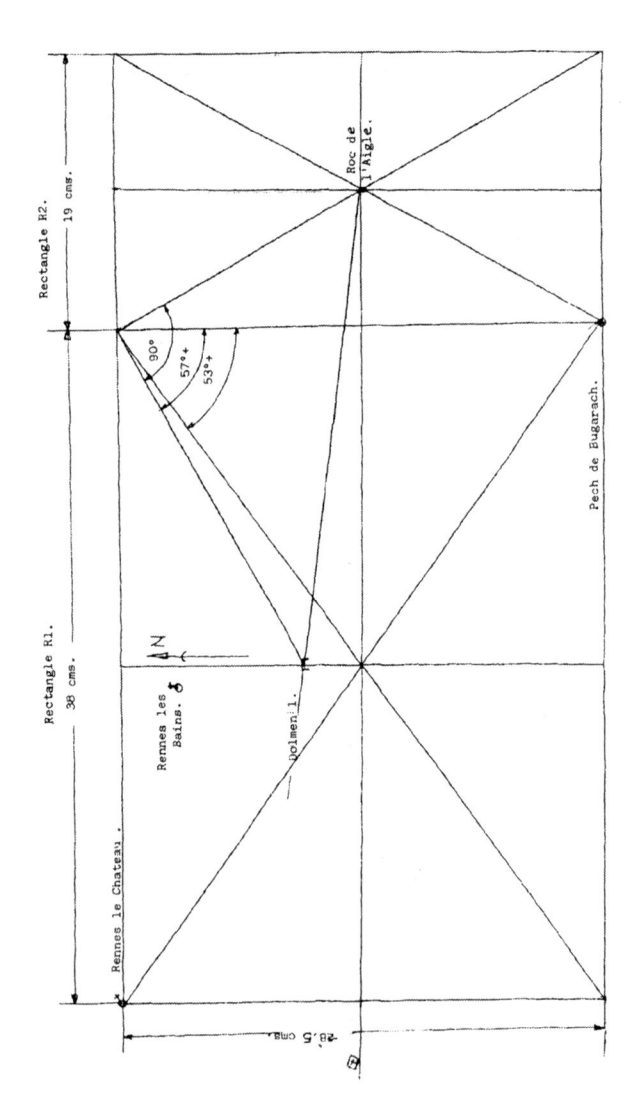

N.T.S.

Rectangle R1. — 38 cms.
Rectangle R2. — 19 cms.
28.5 cms.

Rennes le Chateau.
Rennes les Bains.
Polmeril.
Roc de l'Aigle.
Pech de Bugarach.

90°
57°+
53°+

N

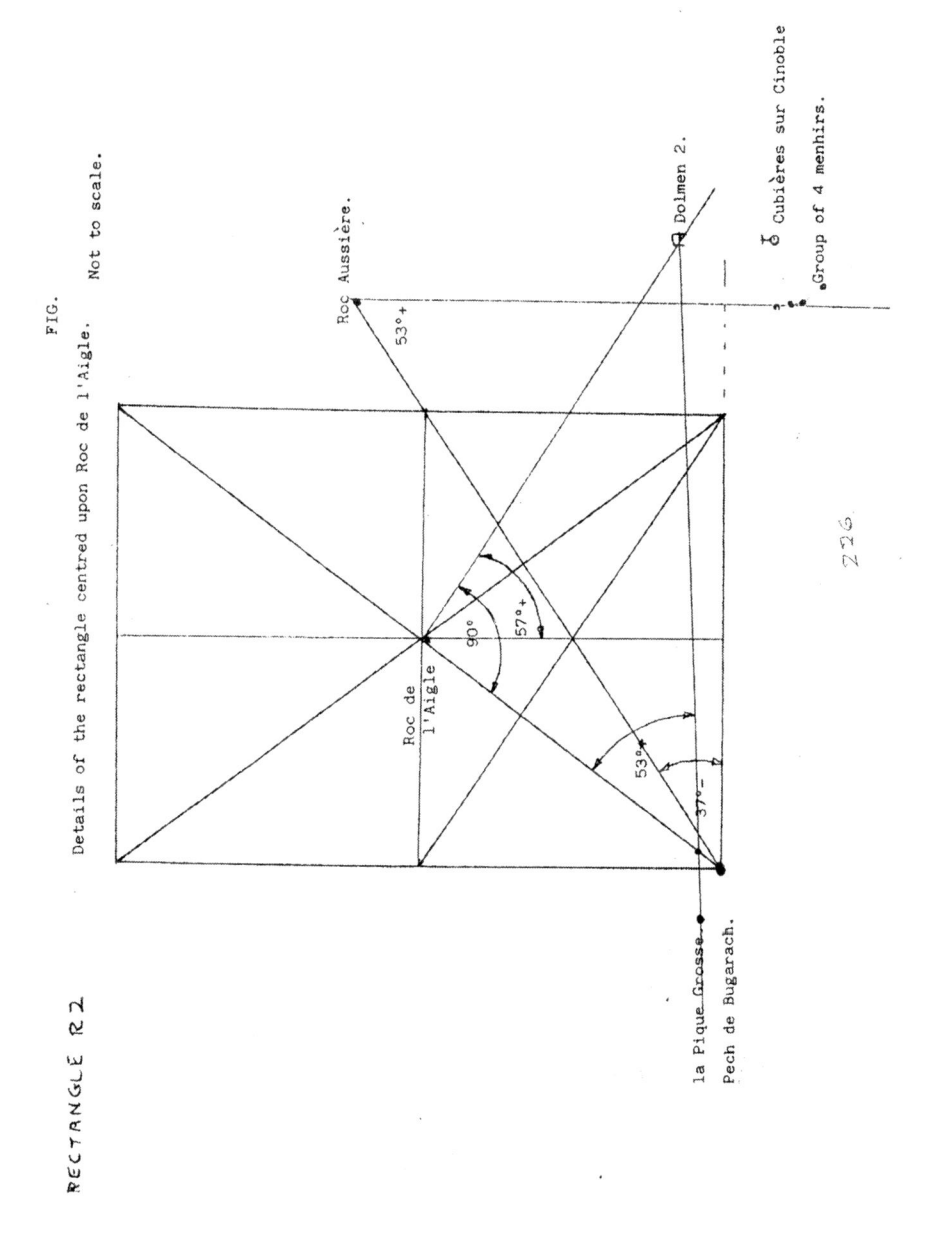

RECTANGLE R2

FIG.

Details of the rectangle centred upon Roc de l'Aigle.   Not to scale.

171

same proportions, for the new map. This indicated that it was slightly larger than the old map, in both directions and by the same amount whether east to west or north to south. It also, quite clearly, retained the rectangle's 3:4:5 proportions for it's triangles. . I suggest that you make reference to the enclosed diagram to avoid confusion that might arise in that which is to follow, step by step.

I have a rectangle with diagonals, plus that which I shall introduce as Dolmen 1 (one), which lies to due-north of the rectangle's central intersection-point. Chance? I found no profit in any extension of the two-point alignment as such But an horizontal line, through the diagonals' intersection-point, when extended to east and west, cutting the rectangle into precise halves, brought a reward that I could not have anticipated.

This third horizontal line, taken a little outside the rectangle to west, hit the southern-most tip of the cemetery-boundary at the village of Granés. I shall be dealing with cemeteries at greater length. The same horizontal line, when extended outside the rectangle to east, makes contact with the northern side of Roc de l'Aigle, Eagle Rock. I wasted no time upon why this might be.

I repeat that any triangle, with sides with ratios of 3:4:5, must reproduce the same three angular values, of which one is 90°s.

My circular protractor indicated angles of arc at 53+ and 57- degrees within the framework of the rectangle. By calculation, employing the 28.5 and 38.0 figures (it matters not the unit of measure), I achieved an answer of 53.130l02°s. With sides in those proportions it cannot be otherwise. The remaining angle would be 36.869898°s.These I shall refer to as 53+°s and 37-°s upon the diagrams.

For need of confirmation I assume that my Dolmen 1 does exist to south of Rennes les Bains. The map shows a series of stars running roughly east to west across the ground to south of that village. A line drawn due to north, from the rectangle's centre-point, cuts across one of those markers, one that is a little different in shape.

The map's legend refers to the stars as being Tas de Cailloux, or English heaps of stones, somewhat similar to ancient boundary-markers. I queried their history when in that area of the Aude but it was a case of they have always been there. Today they are largely concealed among forest trees. Nevertheless, such heaps of stones cannot be of any extensive size due to their inclination to fall and roll around when heaped too high. How large, I asked? The answer was a conventional French shrug of the shoulders, to be expected when precise knowledge is lacking, pursed lips, hands spread apart to indicate somewhere in the region of a metre, in diameter, one assumed.

The second dolmen is registered upon the map, well to it's south-east. For simplicity of reference I designate this as Dolmen 2.

The irregularity in position of those Tas de Cailloux does not favour them as markers for areas of land. Wide-spread as they are, their number is quite impressive. Some are grouped whilst others remain single.

Dolmen 2, or D2, lies to north-east of the village of Cubières sur Cinoble, at the south east corner of the map..

The question will arise as to how certain unnatural landscape features came about in the most convenient of places?

Compared with the megaliths, of Stonehenge, any local modifications, in the vicinity that concerns us, would appear insignificant, with the exception of pre-historic Earthworks, of which there are plenty in the region of the Aude. Our own Silbury Hill is of artificial construction, and covers five acres (two Hectares) of land. The Passage-graves, of Western Europe, required the positioning of immense slabs of stone that no ordinary JCB could lift for all it's hydraulic power.

Here, when necessary, earth might be removed for some distance, surrounding rock leaving it exposed for guidance purposes, a signpost to somewhere of importance. Col de Paradis; what delightful names one finds around the two-Rennes area. One has The Valley of God, The Devil's Armchair, Dead Man, Trembling Rock, Smoking Rock, and many others of pleasing note.

Col de Paradis has a nearby outcrop of rock which is brushed by the eastern vertical of a further rectangle that I select to dub R2, with the first rectangle as R1. With another possibility in mind I extended all three horizontal lines from R1 to eastward enabling me to form a second rectangle that is exactly half the length of the first one, with Roc de l'Aigle at it's centre. It's diagonals fit nicely around this rocky outcrop.

That Col de Paradis nearby outcrop of rock has, to south-east, a single menhir. A line, from this menhir, passing through the south west corner, of Sougraigne cemetery, precisely parallels one of the R1 diagonals. Some might argue that a two or three-element alignment has far less authority than one of a greater number. I normally apply an equal amount of caution, but I would remind them that, in this form of survey, only two points are required for a visual observation. And when such arrangements occur to provide a line that is in keeping with the overall geometric figure, it should not be cast aside without further examination, for it might finally be of value in an understanding of the whole. .

These are not of those more-loosely based Ley-lines. I am, in fact, dealing with a finer degree of layout, the result of which exercise brings to light astonishing designs that could only be due to human intent. I feel convinced that, as we progress, you will accept that human brains calculated the final outcome. In this I continue to stand by my own set rule that all features, which control this geometric pattern must only provide visual observation along a side or corner, for one cannot see through menhirs nor large outcrops of rock. In the region of the Languedoc lie the remnants of numerous dolmens, all part of a sweep that leads toward Marseille. It is important to recall that a French archaeological researcher discovered that they are all aligned with major sun-positions upon the horizons. Why then a sparsety of dolmens in this vicinity. I suspect that, with so many villages scattered across the region, the Church organized a wholesale removal of such permanent reminders of the pagan past.

The D1 diagonal, running to the top right corner, of R1, produces there an angle of near to 57°s. Mere words are inadequate to describe a mounting number of surprises.

With the Dolmen 1 position incorporated with the RI top, right corner to include the Roc de l'Aigle point, one has the making of a right-angled triangle, also the result for a 3:4:5 triangle.

Further calculations indicated that Dl, when viewed from that R1 north-east corner, lay upon a winter solstice sunset azimuth for an early era.

Roc de l'Aigle, R2 rectangle, held yet more reasons for surprise. I commenced by penning a line from Roc de l'Aigle through the second dolmen, D2.. This, in conjunction with R2's diagonal, in the low left quarter, and a line taken through that diagonal to hit La Pique Grosse 1081M spot-height, gave yet one more 3:4:5 right-angled triangle. I was, by then, forcing myself to avoid becoming blasé in relation to each new discovery, revelations of astonishing proportions.

When taken in association with the R2 centre-point a vertical line passing through it, dolmen D2 lies upon a winter-solstice sunrise azimuth for the same era as that of dolmen Dl, the angle being 57°s+, once more. Leaping ahead by a few millennia, this solstice azimuth has been retained, in precisely the same number of degrees, as another which incorporates sides of four Christian cemeteries. When supplanting signs of earlier sacred sites with those of their own religion, Christian believers clearly, and unknowingly, failed to totally eraze shades of paganism beneath their feet.

Once again I referred to the map, checking for other landscape features that might add confirmation indicating that my efforts, to date, rested upon solid foundations.

Not far from Roc de l'Aigle, to its general west, is a group of four small star-symbols upon the map. In future I shall refer to such stars as symbols for heaps of stones or cairns. Relative to one another, those cairns form a rough east/west line. A line, from Roc de l'Aigle, set to reach dolmen Dl, passes along that group of four to hit a neighbouring cairn.

When measuring the sides of a triangle, incorporating dolmen Dl, Roc de l'Aigle and the top corner of R1, I achieved the following in centimetre lengths: 17.2, 22.9 and 28.6. This information I employed in order to calculate one of this triangle's angles opposite to that of 90°s. Since in any triangle with sides in proportions of 3:4:5 units of measure, must have angles opposite to that of the 90°s angle, of 53.130103 and 36.869898°s without fail, it suited my purpose.

I accepted that, under the circumstances 53.09°s was an acceptable confirmation of such a 3:4:5 triangle.

In similar fashion the dolmen D2, which involves the Pique Grosse spot-height, did produce a reasonable outcome.

Roc Aussière lies to east, outside the R2 rectangle. Nothing enigmatic about that until……

A line, from Pech de Bugarach, drawn to pass through the horizontal that divides the rectangle into two equal parts, where it touches the eastern vertical, traces a path directly to Roc Aussière, the angle so-formed being another of 53+°s. A vertical, taken to due south from that Roc, runs through three of a group of four cairns to west of Cubières sur Cinoble. When the baseline, of the R2 rectangle is extended to east, it produces yet another 90°s angle, as in one with sides in ratios of 3:4:5.

Can so many instances, of such geometric exactitude, be a result of coincidence? It cannot be purely by Chance that Dl and D2 fit so neatly into the wider arrangement, with solstice azimuth alignments and the part that they play in reproduction of so many of those triangles. However, it remains remarkable that the overall

Grand Design relies upon so few landscape reference-points in its establishment.

For what it may be worth, dolmen Dl aligns with possible remains of another dolmen.

I checked all alignments with a length of the finest available of thread stretched taut from point to point. I reproduced all lines with a super-fine mapping-pen upon sheets of clear acetate-film held fast in position.

During a visit to Rennes le Château and environs I noticed how extensive was the forest, trees growing to the tops of ridges, and other heights, adding considerably to local elevations. My immediate thought was that this would create a screen against any search for potential, observable alignments.

When walking in part of the forest, I saw that the trees were relatively young. This was confirmed by a French acquaintance who informed me of wide-spread afforestation that took place there, during the mid 1930's.

One hundred years ago Abbé Bérenger Saunière, of Rennes le Château, would not have encountered so vast a barrier to lines of sight. Nor would much-earlier peoples in that vicinity.

I have left unexplored other such possibilities, I did make mental note of two, in particular, potential alignments which come from outside to have connections with the RI and R2 rectangles.

A further point, that I consider to provide worthwhile examination, involves the Fontaine Salée a little to south-west of Roc de l'Aigle, with the aptly-named River Sals running nearby.

It is Fontaine Salée's source of natural salt that gives the river its name, with Sel being French for Salt, with Salière a Salt-cellar. Some ancient tribe probably kept permanent guard over so valuable a source of wealth, to become it's wholesalers and distributors.

To south were passes leading to marsh-land and the wild-life that it sustained.

Taken in conjunction, every earthwork and Tas de Cailloux should bear examination. To the map's south-east close to Camps sur l'Agly and Cubière sur Cinoble, with surrounding area, is much of prehistoric interest awaiting inspection. And so to a later exploration of a landscape.

Other Prehistoric Alignments.

I again introduce that dolmen Dl, with more that points to confirmation that it is of far-more importance than any heap of stones might attract.

Many examples of extensive earth-works, of a pre-historic nature, litter the map with uncommon frequency, these fresh elements, through dolmen Dl, are most impressive. Each of them commences with a spot-height set upon such an earth-work.

To either side of dolmen Dl are more cairns, Tas de Cailloux that form an irregular line running along roughly east to west. This deviation, from the straight, may have been deliberate in order to accommodate various other alignments to pass through a relatively-crowded focal-point.

From spot-height 531M, at Borde d'en Salve, a line picks up Pech de la Roque's spot-height 534M, prior to lining up with a 416M spot-height, then Dl, then two more cairns farther to east.

From Sarrat de la Bézu earth-works spot-height, 413M, this alignment picks up two cairns, Dl, two-more cairns and finally, Roc de l'Aigle.

The Casteillas earthwork, spot-height 502M, commences an alignment passing through dolmen Dl, the triangulation-point at Pech de Rodés, also set upon an earth-works, and a further cairn. Pech de Rodés also assists in the creation of another alignment eastward to two rock-features, those of Roc Aussière and Roc de la Castille.

Of some interest is a group of alignments sharing a common intersection-point at a single cairn. Here, one commencing at Coustassa church, cuts through the Pech Auriol spot-height 545M, to hit Fauteuil du Diable, a sole cairn that provides a start-point for another alignment that passes through two cairns at Soulane to extend onward to Roc de l'Aigle.

The three earthworks, where alignments commence, all lie roughly to south of Rennes le Château.

I, when checking for alignment accuracy, stretch a finest of available thread along them, it's thinness an important factor in this.

Alignments through Dolmen 1.

Crosses represent Menhirs.
Dots represent significant Spot heights.

Rennes les Bains.

Dolmen 1.

Roc de l'Aigle.

817 M. Pech de Rodes.

le Castellas.
502 M.

Sarrat de la
Bezu.
413 M.

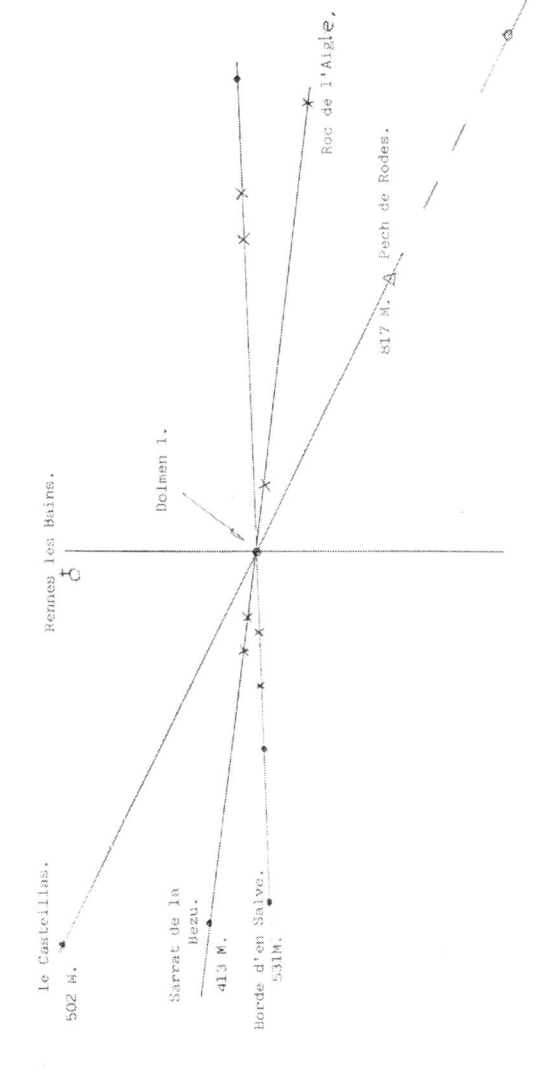

Horde d'en Salve.
531M.

Some short-distance alignments based upon a sole menhir (cairn) a little to north of Dolmen 1.

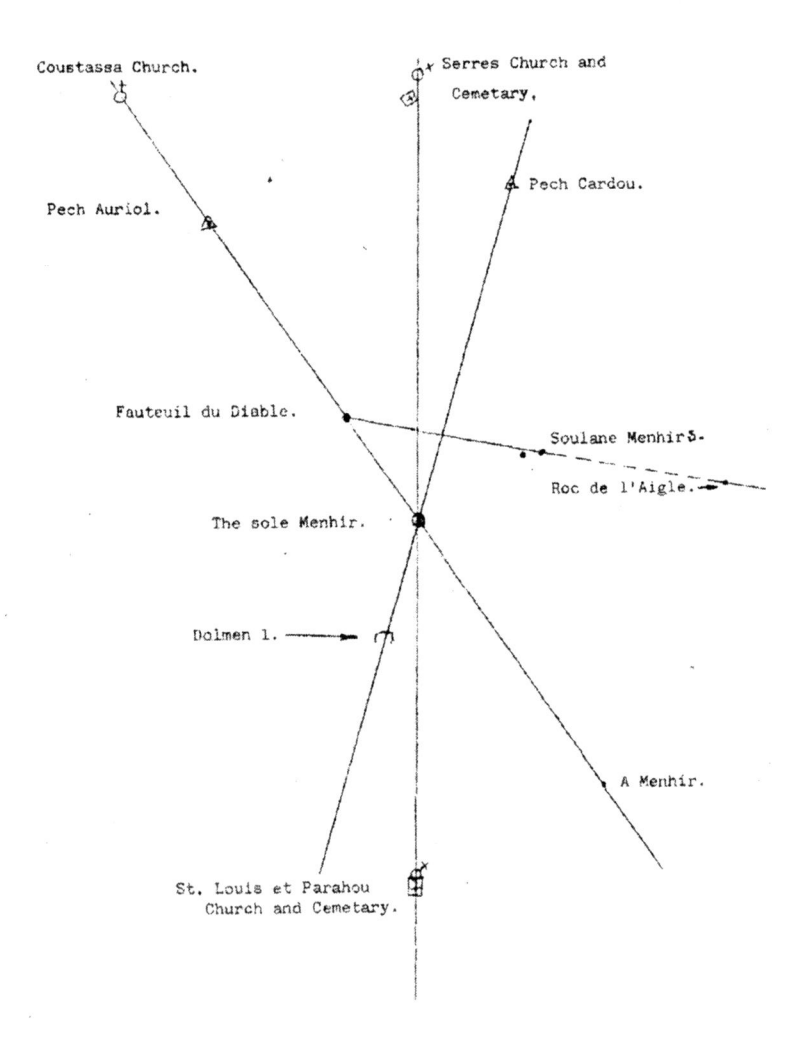

Coustassa Church.

Serres Church and Cemetary.

Pech Auriol.

Pech Cardou.

Fauteuil du Diable.

Soulane Menhirs.

Roc de l'Aigle.

The sole Menhir.

Dolmen 1.

A Menhir.

St. Louis et Parahou Church and Cemetary.

182

Pentagonal Hints.

Pentagrams are associated with goddess figures from antiquity, as are pentacles to be linked with witchcraft. The esoteric origins of pentagrams belong with the planet Venus that reaches five distinctive apogees seen against the night sky, it's five farthest points from Planet Earth in near to every eight years. Both Henry Lincoln and David Wood, in their respective Rennes le Château related books, describe pentagonal geometry across the surrounding landscape. Among other graffiti to be seen at the village of Bugarach lying to south-east of Rennes les Bains, is a number of pentacles.

All angles of a pentagram are divisible by 18°s, exactly, 36, 54, 72 and 108. Of these 54 is not precisely divisible by 12. I wondered could there be other examples of at least an apparent pentagonal influence across the same landscape? I again employed the Pech de Bugarach triangulation-point as the first controlling element.

One feature, upon the map, possibly relative to the local mystery, is the remains of a once impressive château, that of the Knights Templar, in the le Bézu vicinity. From my Pech de Bugarach east/west line, a circular protractor centred upon the triangulation-point, the Château ruins rested against an 18°s line. Beyond that ruin an extension of the alignment touched against the cemetery boundaries of first Le Bézu then Granés. Further, in a clockwise direction, a 36°s sighting took in a peak, that of La Pique, 582M. Similarly a 54°s alignment touched the Cassaignes cemetery-boundary.

I now had some encouraging alignments.

Cemeteries, of this region in general, are widely scattered. They vary in size and boundary-shape and, who knows why, are frequently placed at some distance from their mother-churches, geographically isolated from them. Some belong to mere hamlets.

As I progressed I was forced to seek alignments that ran alongside cemetery-boundary sides or corners, thus forced to follow my own rule that one cannot see through walls of stone, therefore all visual sightings must be made across their outer-surfaces.

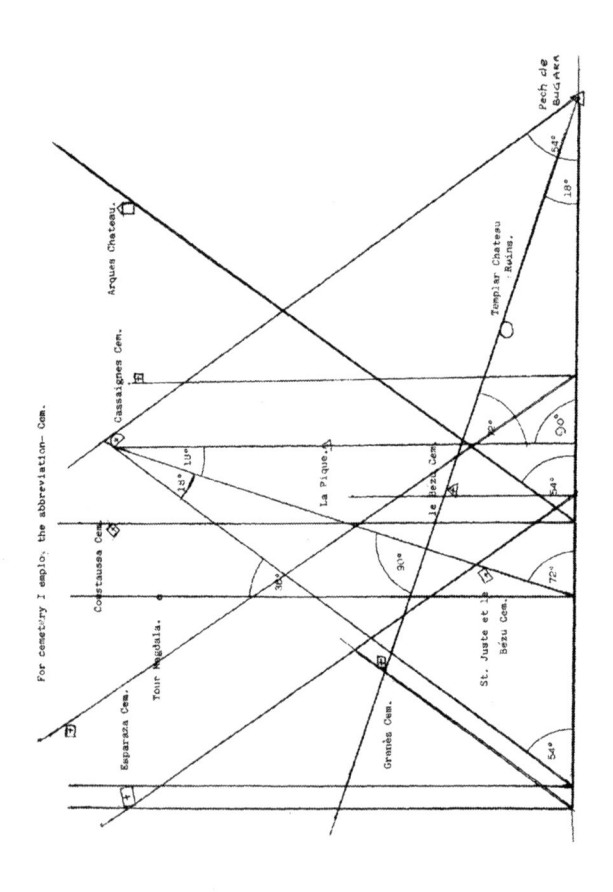

First came a creation of verticals bracketing both sides of a cemetery to be investigated. I commenced with two selections, first, this due to the fact that they rest to north and south of each other, Rennes les Bains and St. Louis et Parahou, their locations. I selected these two because the latter lies to south of the Pech de Bugarach base-line, any verticals bound to cut right through it. It was the eastern, of those verticals, that brought a bonus.

Taking the point, at which that vertical intersects the base-line, a 54°s line, to general north-west hits the north-east corner of a cemetery at Montazels. I do not include diagrams depicting all such alignments.

I moved to a Cassaignes cemetery to be given like treatment. with a 54°s line, from Pech de Bugarach, running against its eastern side that curves to give its boundary a semi-circular form. It was a vertical from it's straight side that, where it touched the base-line, from that point an alignment running to eastward, at a 54°s angle, brings in the Grotte at Arques. However, I wished to maintain only cemeteries in this experiment.

At the same angle a line inclined, from the same base-point, to west, aligns with a corner of a château at St. Sernin village, a longer-range alignment, therefore more-open to question, at 75cms; on the ground 19-kilometres (12 miles).

I wish to impress the fact that these geometric patterns of lines provide only those described, but others remain untested in a wider region.

The Templar Château ruin may well provide a useful vertical, as does Château Blanchefort provide a vertical from which a westward line, inclined at 54°s, runs between twin cemeteries at Autugnac.

Here, again, unlike hunters of Ley-lines, I gave preference to alignments controlled by the same cemetery element. Perhaps the occasional château does intrude but with a linear connection. A spiritual one?

A look at the main diagram reveals some interesting alignments connecting.

Nevertheless, on a broader scale, other features may intrude, such as solitary tombs, also homes for the dead. Some wayside crosses are marked upon the map. Beware of those that are of more-recent date, dedicated to members of the French Resistance who were slain at those spots, during the 1939-45 war with Germany.

Of sixteen cemetery alignments twelve are of eleven kilometres (seven miles) or less in extent, but all of them conforming with that 54°s angle.

Others, of longer distance, are largely acceptable since they conform to the requisite geometry. One which brings in the La Serpent cemetery, might be seen as open to question as perhaps a result of chance. Hmm! French Serpent is masculine, so why feminine LA?

In order to recreate these alignments the use of cemetery sides or corners vastly reduces any possible lee-way which can add to intention upon the part of someone, and to their validity.

I doubt if I all ever fathom out why cemeteries should play so positive a role in the structure of so complex a geometric grid across the landscape. Perhaps in order to gain such awareness one must ignore the controlling part, which they appear to play, and allow thoughts to roam in search of reason. It may rest in a time that precedes Christianity by millennia.

With a Pech de Bugarach base-line moved a mere fraction to north or south, such precision becomes impossible.

There is one metaphysical element which, in general might link them; they all they all represent homes for the dead, their souls long departed Earth. This brings the thought of the original Hallowe'en festival, from a time that precedes that grotesque version, imported from the USA, for monetary gain.

The figure 360 is neatly divisible by 18,36,72 and 90 but not by 54. $360 \div 54 = 6.666666$. Angles of 54°s are to be found in a pentagram. To the north of Pech de Bugarach lies the village of that name. There in the vicinity of the church-yard, are pentagrams inscribed into rock. In company with them are symbols that I believe to direct attention to either cemeteries or churches, probably the former.

I was forced to modify a St. Serin alignment, after giving it a check. Now a tomb replaced the château.

Now here is a thought! Wolfram von Eschenbach, so knowledgeable Templar wise, tells of Grail Castle situated somewhere among the Pyrenees Mountains with the Corbière Range, to be seen as an extension of the former.

Further, from Wolfram, is the hermit -uncle of Parzival, who informs his nephew that *many brave knights dwell at Munsalvaesche. 'Those knights ride out in search of adventure. They do so for their sins, these Templars.*

Members of the Knights Templar brotherhood inhabitted the western and southern Département of Languedoc-Roussillon, a Templar château ruin bearing some witness to this, situated quite near to south of Rennes le Château in our area of the map. They were well established, too, in Pyrenees Roussillon to the south.

In *riding out for their sins* those knights would be bent upon their own salvation. Take Wolframs Munsalvaesch; Mun is mindful of French Mon, perhaps Mont implying Mountain. Sal, the next particle; Running near to, and south of Rennes les Bains, is the River Sals. Here an example of a suspect word given close analysis but difficult to take further. However, Wolfram does bring an element of Arthurian Romance into the Templar era.

Wolfram's Grail is a stone to which he refers as Lapsit Exillis, this generally interpreted as a stone from the heavens. Could this be a piece of meteoric stone? Despite the mystique which has been attached to it might this be a reference to an actual piece of stone?

A little to west of Rennes les Bains there runs a three-element alignment. Commencing at Roc Blanc it passes through Roque Nègre before encountering the Templar château ruin: White Rock, Black Rock and Ruin. To the north of this lies La Pierre Dressée, the Dressed Stone meaning the Upright Stone which proudly stands a little to the north of the road from Arque.

It also fits the 54°s geometry when an inclined line, taken from it, intersects a vertical taken from Tour Magdala at Rennes le Château. If this stone were of meteoric origin we might have heard of it? More for my attention.

Pope Innocent II accused Templars of being un-Christian, with emphasis upon their supposed dabbling in Necromancy. They were, too, similarly censured with worship of skulls, one in particular, gilt with silver, that of a woman, its top hinged to provide access to a smaller female skull in company with two wrapped head-bones.

The Inquisition placed much emphasis upon such *heads* when making charges against the captive Templars, the year 1308. The charge being worship of idols, specifically in the form of skulls with magical properties. Might the accusers unknowingly hit upon a truth? Was there some undetected justification among cemetery alignments? Did Knights Templar, forebears of the accused, site those cemeteries upon pre-historic points of sacred importance, heathen to the Church?

The Languedoc-Roussillon Départment is known for its many ancient dolmens each aligned with positions of importance against sun-rise or set upon the encompassing horizons, unseen by their dead occupants.

One cannot shrug off a possible influence, from the Knights Templar, with casual ease. My investigation of it, in general, leaves me with a feeling that it must contain a powerful female influence, albeit through the figure of Marie Madeleine, or that of a goddess by name one among others, for their positions were all usurped with the arrival of male gods. Between the biblical lines of verse is concealed the second Creation-story concerns, with Eve presented as an evil female tempting poor Adam into an indiscretion, he too entranced to resist her. Poor Adam: poor weak fool. Who then was the stronger? Naturally, the Church of Rome, an all-male company of men bent upon protection of their rich life styles and power, could not permit any return to goddess, in preference to that all-knowing, all-seeing of past, present and future events, Yahweh who, incidentally, as described in the Bible, accepted assistance in the form of hand-maidens supplied by Goddess Lilith, another female to be disparaged by male preachers.

In fact' brief be its biblical presentation, that perpetually-overlooked First Creation, was the work of the Elohim, female deities, of whom Rome's dreaded Astarte/Astoreth is there among them, Astarte whose six-pointed star was to become a Star of David, followed by Solomon in the design of his Seal. *And Hebrews continued to worship in High Places* long after the introduction of Yahweh into their midst. For High Place read Heathen Alter.

And now to an era closer to our own time!

SECOND AGE OF AUDE

HISTORIC

I continue with cemetery-alignments which may appear among those upon Page 184, but now shown individually for sake of greater clarification. I do not doubt that others remain yet to be discovered.

Château Blanchefort.

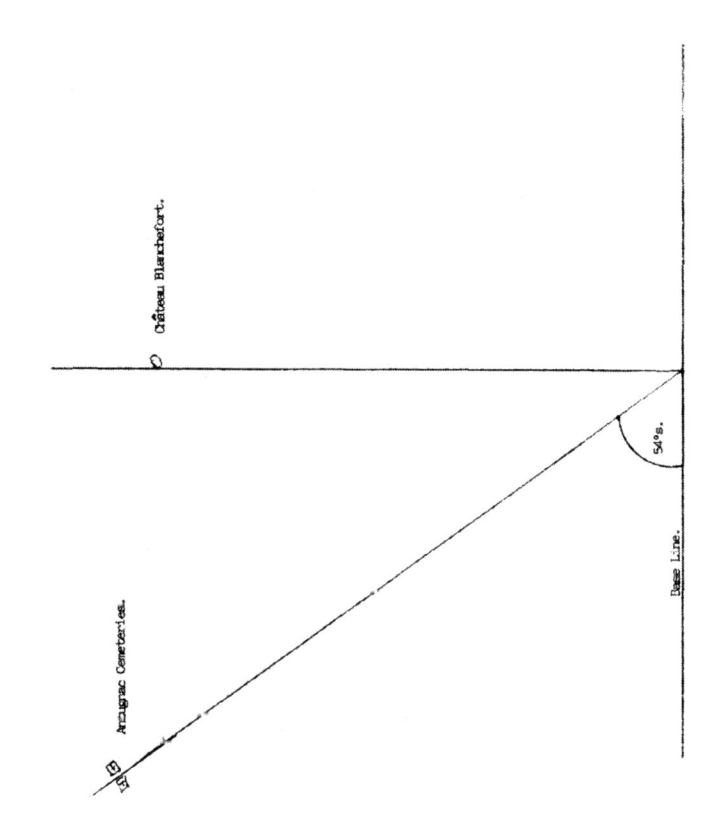

54°s.

Base Line.

Arcagnac Cemeteries.

Cemetery.

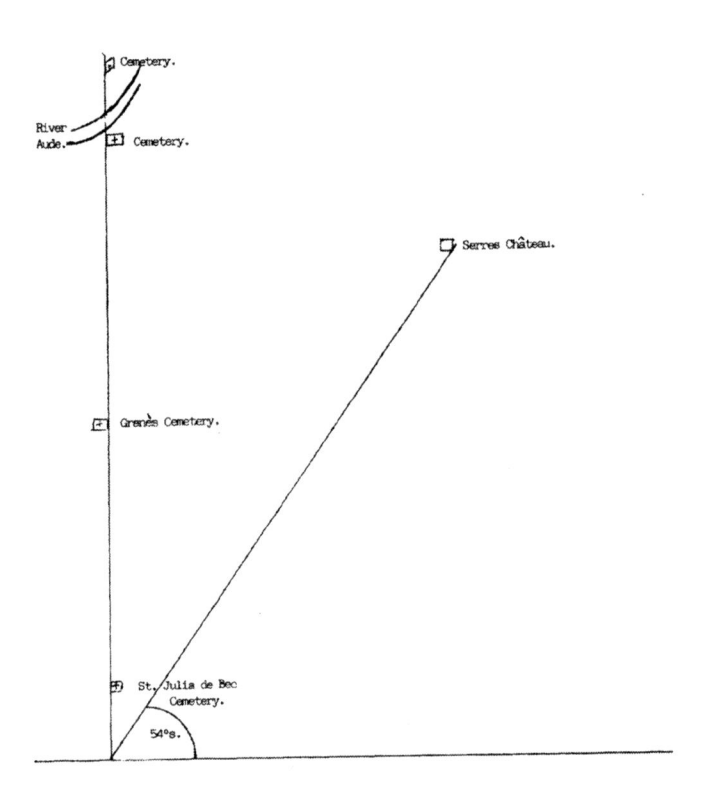

River
Aude. — Cemetery.

Serres Château.

Granès Cemetery.

St. Julia de Bec
Cemetery.

54°s.

Montazels.
River Aude.

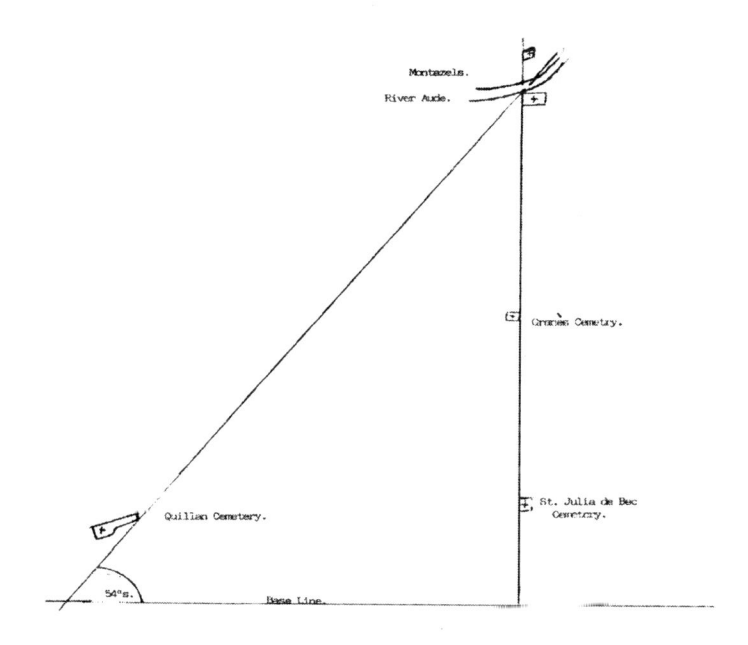

Granès Cemetery.

St. Julia de Bec
Cemetery.

Quillan Cemetery.

54°s.   Base Line.

Fig: La Serpent Geometry.   Not to scale.

○ la Serpent Château.

✠ Rennes le Château.

✠ Rennes les Bains.

54°s.   54°s.   Base Line.

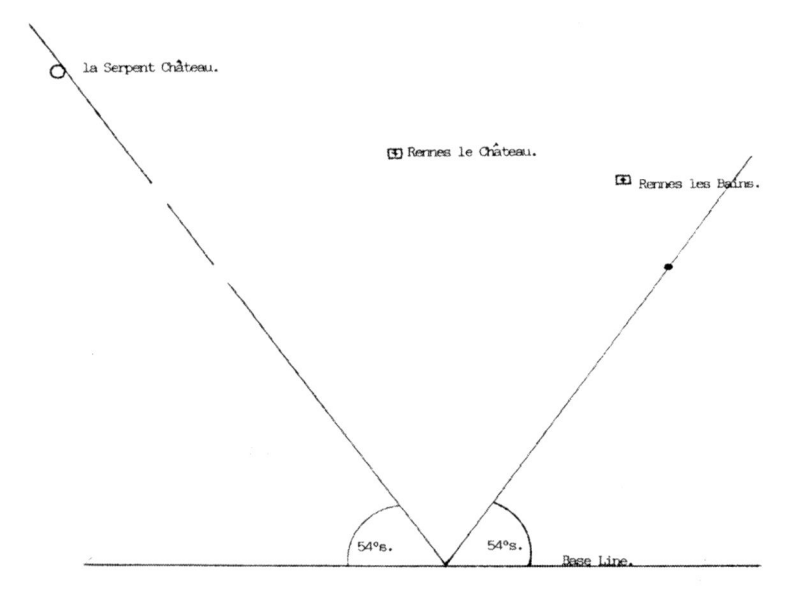

Rennes le Château.   Fig: To Scale.   Rennes les Bains.

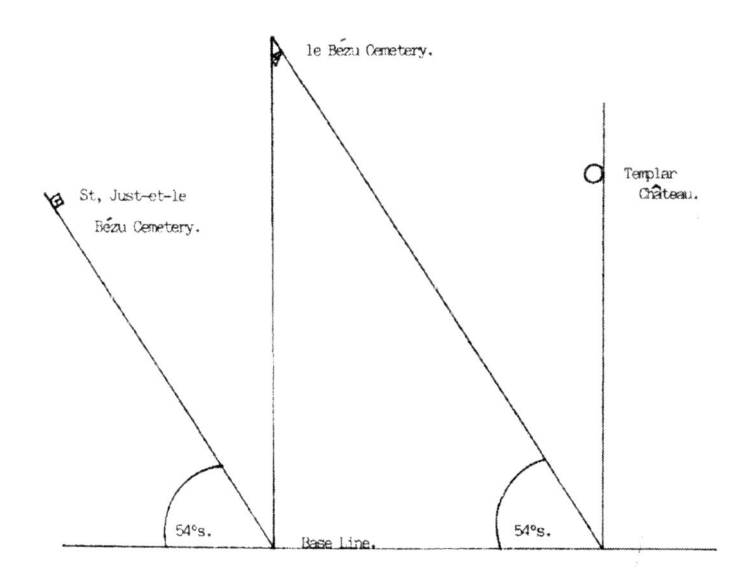

le Bézu Cemetery.

St, Just-et-le Bézu Cemetery.

Templar Château.

54°s.   Base Line.   54°s.

And my bewilderment, too, is severely rocked.
Upon Reflection!
Evidence in white, red and black.

As the subject of Atlantis concerns a sea somewhere and, therefore. sea-going vessels of early years, one can never assume that a ship's captain is not guilty of exaggeration or even downright lies. One may find such a person, without even a hint of a smile from his lips, tell that the ocean outside the pillars of Heracles/Hercules, shall one attempt to transverse it, is so full with mud, huge areas of impenetrable seaweed, plus inevitable demonic monsters breathing stinking fire, which he knew from experience that near to four months were required to reach the other, far continent, often with lack of wind to fill the sails, yet another curse to hinder an honest sailor. Forgive me my dubious reaction to such tales as were banded about in order to scare would-be explorers for new sources of merchandise, or lands. They did occur, ancient trade-secrets. Just how could such quite small vessels, of a far distant era, carry sufficient water and food to maintain a crew throughout thousands of ocean miles, even without such obstacles to overcome? Fish and more fish?

Diodorus Siculus makes brief mention of Jason's Argo which he informs us was carried well inland, in the region of Tritonis, Libya when a series of Western-Mediterranean earthquakes took place. He also brings attention to what appears to be the Scilly isles, with a Greek name of Cassiterides, this in relation to the traffic in tin and copper from nearby Cornwall. He tells us how local people worked the tin by digging it out from between rocks, the resultant product beaten into cube like shapes then, at low tide, taken across for storage at an Island called Ictis, today's St Michael's Mount, the metal there in abundance.

To Ictis come merchants to purchase the tin from the natives then to travel for thirty-days across Gaul, to the mouth of the Rhone by horse.

Diodorus, at least in part is quoting Herodotus 450 BC. He who writes of events some 250 years before his own birth. Strabo confirms the Greek name for the Scilly Isles as Cassiterides as does Pliny.

Diodorus also mentions how, due to a soft climate, the Scilly Isles became known as The Fortunate Isles.

From early times Cornwall seems to have received merchants from Brittany and the Mediterranean vicinity, seeking tin, copper, too. With the arrival of the Middle Bronze-age, circa 1450 BC, sea-trade, with Cornwall appears to have been vastly reduced, this when over-land routes were now employed for movement of tin and copper to cross the Channel en route to the region of the Adriatic, with the Greece-to-be-country nearby. In the Late Bronze-age, around the year 1000BC, came a sharp renewal in trade for Cornwall, it's tin-trade flourishing. This 1450BC date closely coincides with the disaster that overwhelmed Crete.

Incidently, with what might be classed as Divine assistance, or Mother Nature's help, Jason and crew managed to get their vessel back to the waters of the Mediterranean Sea. Take away such awful monsters as Scylla and Charybdis, and the Argonauts' journey becomes a reality.

Someone knew of the Messina Strait off Sicily where dwelt the Scylla, once a lovely maiden transformed into a six-headed monstrosity that would stretch out long necks to seize unfortunate sailors in each of her gaping mouths. Cilla. An unfortunate sobriquet, Cilla.

On the other hand, or side of the Strait, an equally-terrifying Charybdis lurked, living in a gulf from whence three-times per day, it would cause a great chasm to form into which sea-water poured then was disgorged to form savage whirlpools, each inrush of water drawing any nearby vessel to be totally engulfed.

The waters of that strait can be indeed dangerous in reality.

Modern investigation has revealed that, minus the monstrous

obstacle course, the passage of the Argo could be based upon fact, this to include the use of a sheep-skin for trapping gold from a flowing stream, the Golden Fleece.

With the ending of the last Ice-age commencing 12,000 years ago, with ice spreading to 1600 metres in thickness across northern and southern continents, reaching to Denmark and much of the British Isles, in the northern hemisphere, with similar inroads into southern continents, the seas would have been greatly reduced in area and depth, land-masses correspondingly increased, although largely devoid of flora and fauna.

Yet another tale tells of sea-god Poseidon who angrily causes the inundation of Attica, Argolis, Rhodes and the whole Mediterranean coast passed Sicily, this being the Deucalion Flood, a folklore recollection of an actual tidal-wave, of tsunami type doing the damage here?

Escaping from one potential disaster to be faced by another, the Argonauts lay at anchor on Dicte where a bronze giant hurled bombs of stone their way. A description of how Medea rid them of this monster is mindful of a volcanic upheaval.

The monster's blood began to flow like molten lead accompanied by a great noise of cracking. As the Argonauts sailed away a terrible veil shrouded the sea. Lava flows, earthquakes, volcanic eruption?

The volcanic fault-line through the Mediterranean Sea, caused by the African Plate rubbing against that of Eurasia, branches off through Sicily to follow a northerly route to west of Italy, this in the general direction of the French Puy de Dome craters which lie, in world-related distance, not so far from the earthquake zone of the Roussillon region of that country, with the major fault-line running to westward passed the Golfe du Lion to its north.

Of course, the Etna and Vesuvius continue alive in our day.

So, in order to dissuade others from learning their secret locations, promising gain, in whatever the form, merchant sea-men would invent frightening stories of obstacles to be faced, deadly-enough to cause the deaths of those who would wish to venture in a certain direction by ship, or previously untraveled land.

Human feet must have left their mark upon the Azores Islands, as those temple stones indicate. Whose?

Phoenicians might be favoured, yet their history reveals that they were not in the habit of leaving lasting impressions of their passing. Whether or not that might be due to their homeland being a narrow strip, along the coast of Syria, where food may not have been easy to grow in abundance, where, in order to deter arrival of strangers, drawn by visible signs of farming communities with food, they tended to follow a nomadic style of existence.

The Phoenicians built ships in Lebanese cedar, so they may be expected to do this in situ, with the Lebanon becoming their centre for naval excursions around the Mediterranean Sea. They were literate people with their own non-vowel alphabet which, as a precursor to the Greek and our own version with vowels of today. Robert Graves proposed that the version used by us, is derived from an Egyptian source with a strong influence from the Aegean.

With their own mercantile marine Cretan Minoans preceded the Phoenicians in that respect, they who traded with Egypt, they whose Linear A and Linear B archaic forms of script from which is derived the Greek alphabet.

Commencement date for the Cretan culture is uncertain but, in accordance with some authorities, it at least parallels that of Egypt, Mesopotamia and Sumeria with a provisional date of 2600 BC.

Thus to the colours white, red and black.

These I remind you, are colours of stone used at Atlantis for construction of sacred buildings, according to Plato. They are representative of the Cretan Triple Goddess as white for Virgin

Maiden, red for Nubile Woman and black for Wise Crone, and of an appropriate nature, one might accept.

There exist attempts to directly associate the Hesperides with Atlantis upon the west coast of Africa. With no apparent sign of an earthquake zone.

Sir James Frazer makes reference to the Hesperides in his The Golden Bough, but here they relate to a sanctuary for Hyppolytus of former Greek origins a god-like hero who dies beneath the hooves of wild-horses. This sanctuary to Hyppolytus, is set among the beautiful Gardens of the Hesperides with its luscious groves of lemon and oranges, tall cypress spearing gracefully upward, the whole overlooked by mountains. Indeed a veritable Atlantis, one might believe. It was located where Poseidon's sacred isle rises from the sea, its peaks shrouded with the sombre, green of pines. I have no further details of that sacred isle.

My own thoughts concerning the Greek Hesperides became rooted long in the past, with an idea that, famed for it's Golden Apples, it lay well to west, perhaps the Iberian Peninsular, yet another Elysian Fields, Isles of the Blessed type of setting, yet another Hereafter of apple orchards where dead heroes live forever in a land of wine, women and song. Wherever, in such a context, there is mention of apples one should consider such a fruitful illusion.

In the aftermath of Thera's monumental eruption no lives appear to have been lost among a population with a *Minoan* bloodline, they who seem to have sufficient forewarning of that impending disaster. Ships, carrying them to safety, would be likely to head for mainland colonies, their trading-posts, whilst others, from the later Cretan calamity, could escape by sea upon a fleet of vessels already in safe harbours or still out to sea. They were accustomed to longer voyages with destinations such as Egypt where they had flourishing trade. But....

Expert promulgation of extensive-in-height tsunami, this assumed to follow the Thera eruption, judged by evidence such as occurred in Indonesia and elsewhere with sea-shores nearby, the results of far-less powerful volcanic activity, did not happen, nor was the Isle of Crete inundated by metres-in-height walls of sea-water from the same source.

In order to learn more upon this subject may I suggest that you read Eberhard Zangger's excellent The Future of the Past: Archaeology of the 21st. Century. It provides historical continuity, in the region of the Aegean and Asia Minor from the earliest of times.

There is a second *but* to be added. It now follows.

But how does one sustain an argument that an Atlantis, which appears to increase in proportion to become a huge continent, suggested to be greater in area than both Libya and Asia placed together, that lay within the Atlantic Ocean, conceivably to accept as a reality, for it to sink suddenly beneath the waves, the Azores a mere vestige of that former land?

The Azores rest atop a part of the Atlantic Ridge, standing at 9 kilometres, (6-miles), in height, a mountain greater in height than Mount Everest. Surely so huge a disturbance would have altered the face of the planet, by so staggering an amount that it would be archeologically detectable today, far more noticeable than a few small islands thrusting through the present ocean surface?

Yet another *but*!

But it is now confirmed that no immense tsunami swamped the Isle of Crete when Thera blasted the global atmosphere in so dramatic a fashion. In fact there was no tsunami travelling in any direction at that time.

At about 1470 BC fires broke out across Crete, none of them due to hot ash falling from any volcanic eruption, so it appears. I have a suggestion that may or may not explain how that catastrophe came about.

Extended spells of dry weather often produce forest or crop-fires. If in an earthquake zone any even minor eruption might commence a conflagration which, once started, takes on unstoppable proportions, the land so-engulfed, left black, bare of edible sustenance, famine extensive.

Under those conditions survivors, with available ships, would leave hoping to reach more-favourable shores.

At the time of the Thera eruption it's *Minoan* settlers, with mainland settlements, their mercantile fleet perhaps scattered but still available for future needs, thus survived long after the event.

I now offer more fundamental speculation and theories founded upon whatever other theme which may attract my lively mind.

Again I came across across the Phoenicians dated to the early-years of the 12th. century BC, this unlike instances, that place them at convenient dates of much-earlier years in order to prove some quaking theory, as often as not relative to an Atlantis outside the Strait of Gibraltar in order to bolster-up yet another piece of journalistic nonsense.

Although there exist conflicting dates, 1630 and 1530 BC, for the Thera eruption(s), I later describe why the latter is now proven to be positively acceptable.

Doubtless, captains of Thera's fleet of ships would find the time to consult one another at a suitable juncture during the course of rescuing the islands inhabitants, to make provisional arrangements for future establishment at a new land far-distant from so vividly an unstable area of the Eastern Mediterranean Sea. As an inventive and sea-faring nation they would wish to continue former occupations, with access to established customers. History repeatedly reveals how people, suddenly uprooted from previous situations, for one of a number of reasons, tend to remain together, tribal instinct too powerful to ignore. It provides that necessary cohesive strength in numbers by which to overcome whatever vicissitudes, both man-made or natural, the future may bring.

Archaeologists have discovered Phoenician coins, circa 500 BC, revealing that these people sailed into the Atlantic Ocean, as far as the Azores islands, at that date. I wondered could *Minoans* have sailed into the Atlantic Ocean, too, although at a much-earlier date. Who knows?

Before going in search of such an undertaking I must return to Plato's discourse upon Atlantis.

Thus we are informed that a Greek army won a battle with invading Atlanteans. The name Greek, of course, is a generic term for inhabitants of that Agean part of the world long before the establishment of a Greek nation. In fact, there were, from 1600-1200 BC, people there, in that territory, whom we know as Mycenaean who, therefore, are to be accepted as Plato's *Greeks,* a people who existed during the latter stages of the *Minoan* culture.

Rather richly-decorated were those Mycenaean palaces, quite rich their occupants as continuing excavations reveal. A question arises as to when the Mycenaean civilization ended, this all due to one of those Dark Ages which archaeologists ascribe to gaps in their endeavors to trace this or that preferable, unbroken history interrupted by a discovery of styles in pottery, resting together, from two different eras. With due apology may I suggest that it is usually a case of one evacuated site being re-occupied centuries later, the land recovered for farming and feeding of livestock.

Stone-walls, in France to north of the area that I later describe, strongly reflect Mycenaean workmanship. This awaits clarification.

Might those stone-walls, of possible Mycenaean construction, be Atlantean? I very much doubt it!

As for ships, that venture outside the Pillars of Heracles, thought to be Atlantean, discoveries of boat-remains, in the general vicinity of the Mediterranean Sea, some also seen upon antiquated inscriptions, too, show that even before 3000BC, trade in volcanic obsidian occurred along the coastal regions of Greece. To that is to be added evidence, for early sea-going vessels, drawn from below sea-level, including the North African region, long prior to Plato's Atlantis era. There was, too, some type of trading by sea, along the Iberian Peninsular, and Bay of Biscay, all the way to Scotland, 3000BC.

In parallel with the abandonment of Crete, by its *Minoan* inhabitants came a time when foreign trade, by visiting ships, suddenly decreased in Cornwall.

Landscape Geometry of the Aude, again.

The Aude vicinity of French Languedoc-Roussilon contains a number of features that Plato included in his Atlantis dialogue, they being stone in the colours of white, red and black, a saline fountain, springs of water both hot and cold, a mountainous background and even former mines of gold, all of which are to be found in reality within or relatively near to the area covered by that rectangular geometry. Not only is this an earthquake-zone it also has what are named d'Al Pouis Craters, as well, although unmentioned by the Greek philosopher, those Mycenaean-in-style, walls in loose stone together with what one might call *Look-out* towers. Who then may have been sufficiently knowledgeable to create those rectangles of earlier pages, set in the substance of eternal stone, with *Fontaine Salée* included, Poseidon's Fountain of Salt? Has anyone else discovered another location that includes those same particular features that echo those of Atlantis? I suggest, tongue in cheek, that the answers might rest with either Minoans, forced by the edicts of Mother Nature from ancestral homelands or by Mycenaean merchant explorers.

Who were the Atlanteans who travelled eastward from *Portugal, Spain or France,* to engage in battle with armed forces of Greeks, a misnomer for Mycenaean occupants of a land to be later called Greece?

A characteristic of shared cultures, for the peoples of Minoan Crete, Spain and France, is the Bull.

Where it concerns a dating, for the rectangles, that must remain, at least for the present time, upon details of them being submitted to someone with enough interest in them to check the two azimuths for their winter and summer solstice alignment angles more accurately than can I.

Today's continuing archaeological exploration of Thera gathers even more evidence by which to expand upon history surrounding the years of that eruption and that part of the world in general.

As quite often occurs, I am concentrating upon the typed word when another fleeting thought interrupts the process of tapping keys upon my computer, this an occasion that drew me toward a second examination of previous results of mathematical exploration. It is called lateral thought should I have forgotten to mention it elsewhere. I learnt to never ignore such mental processes.

You will recall my earlier attempts to establish a year for the destruction of Plato's Atlantis, my answer being only an approximation rooted in the centuries between the lifetimes of Plato and Solon, the two most important characters directly involved with the mystery.

A re-consideration of that attempt brought a decision to think in terms of a year that was less arbitrary, that of the birth of Solon 630 BC. And sometimes one thing leads inexorably to another.

Once more I divided the Egyptian priest's 8000 plus 1000, by 10, the answer 900. To this last figure I added the Solon 630 which created more than a tiny degree of excitement, for $900 + 630 = 1530$, the year BC., for Thera's monumental hiccough, and the date from Egyptian records of great upheavals in Nature, the year given to deposits of Theran pumice along the shores of the Nile Delta. This brings me to believe that archaeologists would find it worth their while to take Atlantis far more seriously.

The earlier year, for Thera's eruption, of 1630 BC., can no longer compete with 1530 BC., due to scientific methods based upon carbon-dating that became suspect due to the amount of carbon ejected during that explosion.

Probe sufficiently deeply and a few agreeable surprises arrive!

A Second Atlantis?

There exists a tantalizing report of a Spanish metropolis, ancient in origin, discovered, by archaeologists, in part beneath the Andalusian city of Jaén. It consists of a central island surrounded by concentric rings of canals and land. Carbon-dating, of a human remains, taken from it, give dates of 2,200- 2030 BC. Further examination of the site suggests it's abandonment before 1500 BC., perhaps a date of great importance with regard to the destruction of Atlantis.

As is frequently the case, former abandoned centres of human occupation are later reconstructed; the Jaén site thus treated a little after the year 1200 BC. This ancient metropolis, clearly visible to later Greeks who gave it the name of Ourignis, as the proverbial crow flies, is 830 kilkometres (520 miles) from the French Golfe du Lion, my favoured Mediterranean location for Atlantis.

In addition to the above is a suggestion that the Jaén Atlantis was constructed to a design for an earlier model. However, the site is too far inland to be surrounded by sea-water, unless an unknown upheaval modified that area of Spain.

At no great distance from Jaén is the city of Sevilla, to south of which lie the Greek Gades, *Spanish Cadiz*, just outside the Gibraltar Strait and Pillars of Heracles, with the region known to Greeks as Tartessos with ample sources of gold, silver, copper there for the mining or direct purchase by visiting merchant-ships. The mineral wealth of Tartessos would have been a secret closely guarded by visiting traders.

The present-day people known as the Basques have, in common with the Atlanteans, no known substantiated origins.

With their territory straddling the Pyranees range of mountains, from France into Spain, proud Basques have a history that begins with a deeply-shadowed distant past, a past in a country that Basques call Atlantika, centred upon the Bay of Biscay.

With an interest in Golfe du Lion Atlantis, naturally, I point out that the present population of Basques spreads to land quite near to that Golfe du Lion.

Their present homeland, centred upon the eastern end of the Pyrenean Range, has a shoreline leading northward to Brittany, the Scilly Isles, Cornwall and Ireland, with those local Lost Isles. There is the Green Isle of the Basques, the llha Verde of the Portugese, the Irish Falias, British Lyonesse, Welsh Avalon, and Celtic Hy-Breasail. All just the one lost island I suggest.

The Basque language has no known origins. Their name for it, Euskara, does, it is said, share possible elements with that of ancient Troy, and with the pre-Roman Etruscans of western Italy.

Mention of the Etruscans brings to mind the daughter of Atlas, he who ruled over western Italy in accordance with old legend, his daughter named Atlantia. There are many variations upon the word Atlantis. A question: following their enforced dispersal by the coming savage forces of Thera's outburst, what became of the *Minoan* population who appear to become lost to us historically? Since the name Minoan is of relatively modern invention, by what are they to be identified by researchers of today? Sea-Peoples of Egyptian records, 1200 BC., appear to be composed of sea-going mercenaries of later arrival as do Phoenicians, who, as a an eventual sea-power, come closer to 800 BC and must be excluded.

With mounts Vesuvius and Etna to remind them of Mother Nature's occasional hiccoughs, Etruscans lived to general north of Libyan Lake Tritonis to west of which, Diodorus Siculus informs us, an awe-inspiring series of earthquakes took place, sufficient evidence for me to place Atlantis in the Golfe du Lion.

Whether of actual name or that imposed during our present era, my choice for an original Atlantean State spreads even more widely with possibilities among Basques, Etruscans, Minoans, Mycenaeans, the peoples of an early Languedoc-Roussillon vicinity, Europeans all. This becomes increasingly feasible when a far-too steeply sided Central Atlantic Ridge, as a home for that continental Atlantis, is no longer tenable.

A Maze of Understanding.

It was not only Phoenicians who had a habit of leaving behind little or no trace of their passing, just as most sea-farers, of ancient times, would go to enormous lengths to maintain the secrecy of their routes taken to sources for valuable merchandise in the form of rare ores, particularly those of gold, silver, copper and tin. How, then, could I, prove, by whatever their personal name among the Mediterranean's various traders by ship, that others had passed westward into the Atlantic Ocean at a very- early date? Say 2000 BC.

I had need of a surfeit of good fortune if I was to succeed with such a perhaps impossible task, no doubt about it. But try I must.

With my mode of research I am not unlike a dedicated archaeologist in that I do have an excess amount of patience upon which to draw, in company with powers for careful observation.

One thing led to another as a result of which I opened a small box, overlooked throughout years. Inside it were three volumes from the 1970's involving ancient mysteries in general. It was the book entitled The World Atlas of Mysteries upon which I was to eventually concentrate my research.

I reached pages 154-158 within the region of 30 depictions, in number, of mazes, some from Britain, some from Western Europe.

The word maze might bring to mind the legend of Theseus, the Cretan Labrynth and the Minotaur and Knossos palace.

At the centre of this maze dwelt the terrible Minotaur, half-man, half-bull to which the City of Athens was forced to deliver seven boys and seven girls, annual sacrifices to the monster.

It was that man of invention, Daedalus employing bronze for his works, who designed the maze with its many twists and turns sufficient

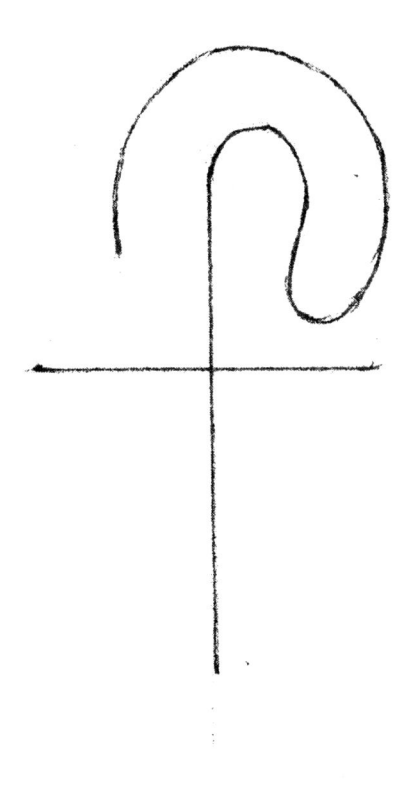

The distinctive entrance/exit design in a Cretan maze.

to disorientate anyone who entered. lost until they would eventually wander into the Minotaur's lair, where it waited for its victims.

Legend informs us that brave Athenian-youth, Theseus, volunteered to become one of fourteen youngsters demanded by Crete, due to be sacrificed to the Minotaur.

An accurate example of the maze impressed upon a Cretan copper-coin discovered during archaeological excavations at the palace at Knossos. Circumstances would date this to pre-1470 BC when fire ravaged the island, perhaps due to deliberate causes, or the savagery of earthwakes. Again the inhabitants appear to have been perhaps forewarned.

Came the day when the chosen youngsters set foot upon the Isle of

Crete, among them Theseus who, upon arrival, immediately fell in love with the king's daughter, Ariadne who, one must assume, reciprocated similar affection for him. Advised by Daedalus the princess spun a long thread by which, playing it out to his rear, Theseus could re-trace a path in reverse, taking him safely out of the maze.

A photograph of the 1960's discovery of a Cretan Maze upon a rock-face at Tintagel, Cornwall, a precise replica of the maze design impressed upon a Minoan coin, circa 2000BC.

For Theseus it was a *game, set and match,* the Minotaur slain, all fourteen Athenian boys and girls returned to safety.

Among my volume's depiction of a variety of mazes was one

impressed into a side of a coin found among excavations at Knossos, Crete.

A reproduction of the Gothland Isle, Gulf of Finland, Cretan Maze, in size 18 metres in diameter, with it's so significant entrance/exit pattern that is only to be seen elsewhere upon the Cretan coin from Knossos and it's Cornish equivalent. Note the two extra paths, the only difference from the original.
The photo-copy appears to have been reversed.

Next to my literal amazement (no intended pun) was yet another maze in design, an exact duplication of the example from Crete.

Discovered only circa 1960, our era, carved into a rock-face upon the northern shore of Cornwall, at Tintagel in fact, is that second Cretan image.

My interpretation of this, with Cornwall a rare and lavish source for precious tin, made easily accessible from between rocks, copper available there too, for production of Bronze, someone from aboard a *Minoan* merchant-ship, had left an indelible *calling-card* or *trade mark*, a badge to be recognized by any future Cretan ship's-captain who came that way for the same purpose as he.

If my theory is acceptable then ships from Knossos must have preceded Phoenician counterparts in passing between the Pillars of Heracles to enter the Atlantic Ocean. It also favours them with the title of Atlanteans.

Never-the-less, there exists surprise in the form of a third such maze which presents a close parallel in design of the Cretan and Cornish equivalents. It lies upon the Isle of Gothland within the Gulf of Finland and is cut into the ground, its diameter is of 18 metres, (60 feet) and, with one exception, is otherwise a demonstrable copy of the other two.

The Gothland maze has, in finger–print terms, two extra whorls but, of inescapable significance, is the pattern of entrance/exit, unique to only these three mazes.

Was it only that *Minoans*, cousins to counterparts on Crete, following the dramatic collapse of their Thera homeland, regroup to become Plato's Atlanteans? Or were they already worthy of that title?

As my placing of Atlantis relies partly upon the records of first-century BC, Greek historian Diodorus Siculus, I felt obliged to seek support for his reliability in that regard. To that end I studied a book entitled Motya; Unearthing a Lost Civilization, by Gaid Servadis, an excellent volume that concerns the city of that title, set upon the isle of Sicily. It improved my confused understanding of how Phoenicians, Punicians and Carthginians inter-related.

Professional archaeologists, of our present era, took over from earlier amateurs' exploration into that lost-city, employing Diodorus Siculus as a textual guide, all in agreement that the Greek historians' records were fully reliable. Of course, Diodorus did rely, in part,, upon the works of such as Greek historian Herodotus. I was pleased to receive confirmation of the reliability of the works of Diodorus. It also gave support for my Golfe du Lion location for sunken Atlantis hypothesis.

Atlantis: the Positive and the Negative

Where it relates to Plato's continental–in-size Atlantis, set in the mid-Atlantic, I feel sufficiently confident to declare this an impossibility for that ocean ridge has sides far too steep for such a land to have rested safely upon it. This forces any factual Atlantis to have been elsewhere, all western Atlantic shores no longer tenable, if ever there were to be seriously acceptable contenders for this research.

Therefore negative.

Large, worked pieces of stone have been found a little below sea-level off Japan and elsewhere worldwide, none of them to be successfully equated with Atlantis.

I, therefore, return to those factors which favour the Golfe du Lion Atlantis.

I, here, take into the reckoning each of those factors, mentioned in Plato's Atlantis dialogue, that can be proven or exist today as duplications of elements from the Greek's description, the positive constituents.

Natural supplies of hot and cold spring-water.

Positive

Shoals of mud that made impossible the passage of ships. This describes what would be likely to occur as a result of a sudden sinking of a land-mass with suitable geographical elements in its structure.

Accepted as probable.

Capable of producing an abundance of edible crops. Immediately to the north and west of Golfe du Lion the Mediterranean climate is well-suited not only to grain-crops but also to the then luxury of vines, peaches, other soft-fruits and many types of vegetable.

Positive

Since the Aude vicinity of Languedoc-Roussillon contains evidence for an earthquake zone, volcanic, too, fits well within the Diodorus Siculus account of a series of earthquakes that occurred within the Mediterranean region to the west of Lake Tritonis in Libya.

Positive

Volcanic activity invariably leaves large deposits that became stone, in the colours of white, red and black, present today in that Aude vicinity.

Positive

With the sumptuous palace of Cretan Knossos as an example, that of Atlantis becomes.

Positive

219

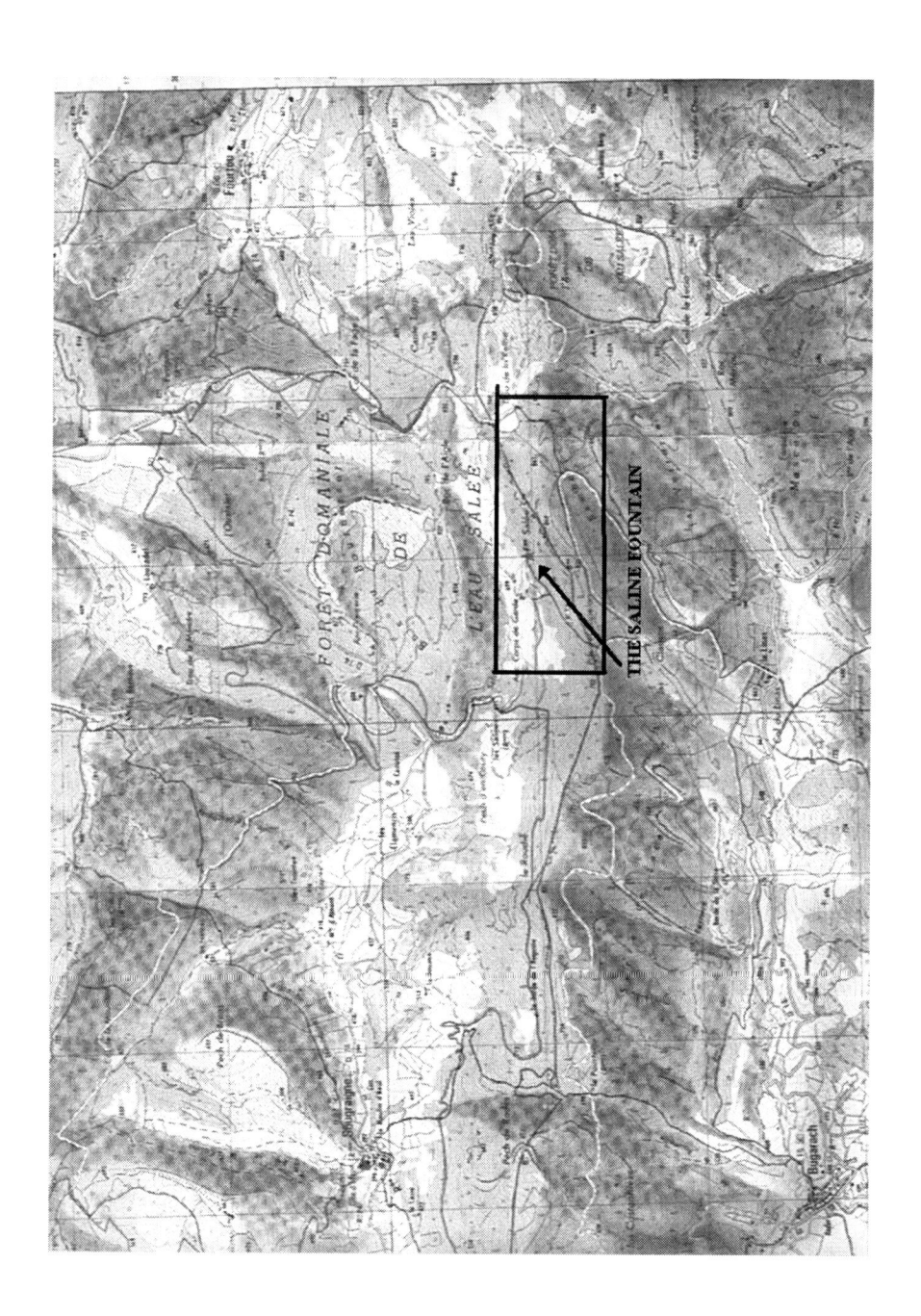

Other features, mentioned by Plato, are lakes, marshes, rivers, mountains and even gold-mines, all of which make up the geology surrounding the French Aude locality, most certainly **Positive**.

Any serious investigator of any topic, selected or thrust upon them, will automatically ask themselves why this or that, often apparently insignificant factor arises among otherwise serious elements?

I return to that saline fountain which was a result in the contest between Athene and Poseidon, otherwise known as Earth-shaker: again I ask why Plato's introduction, of so apparent a non-sequitur? It fails to reveal any note of importance for the Atlantis theme. Or does it do so?

Long before the birth of Plato, Hellenic Greeks had become a major influence in lands around the Mediterranean shores. In the year 330 BC Greek merchant-adventurer, something of a geographer too, Pytheas was sent to sea, from Massalia, French Marseille of today, officially in order to study trade in tin and amber whilst unofficially searching for Plato's Atlantis, described by the latter only a few years previously.

Pytheas' journey took him out from the Meditteranean Sea into the Atlantic Ocean where he turned to northward, his route taking him to Bordeau, Lands End, Cornwall to study the production of tin. He circumnavigated the British Isles, mapping them to within one fortieth of today's estimate, this error possibly influenced in part by changes in sea-levels, and then sailed on to the north for a further six days to Thule and frozen seas, the summer-time edge of the Arctic Circle.

Pytheas is the first known observer, and recorder, of the Midnight Sun and Aurora effect. There are suggestions that he reached an Iceland occupied by a remnant of Neolithic people who sailed along the Polar-route between Scandinavia and Labrador. Although he failed to find Atlantis, Pytheas deserves recognition for what he did achieve. He did, however, meet people who mixed honey with grain to produce their special drink, (alcoholic), lived upon fruit, products of the dairy, and threshed corn inside barns, a happy farming people, no doubt.

Difficult to Disregard.

I made an earlier and brief mention of the Spanish town of Jaén where modern archaeologists discovered remains of an ancient city, the original construction of which bears a remarkable resemblance with the Atlantis as described by Plato. It had a system of six canals in concentric circles, with a central island, all separated by artificial rings of land.

One major problem with this, should one wish to equate it directly with Atlantis, is the fact that it rests some 100 kilometres (60 miles) inland, from the Mediterranean Sea's coastline and, at a height above sea-level, in the region of 800 metres (2400 feet).. Never-the-less, it provides a coincidence that cannot be ignored, without suspicion.

By natural forces, earthquake, maybe volcanic at 1500 BC., this amazing city was severely damaged and abandoned. It was later rebuilt circa 1200 BC.

Spanish expert, Diaz-Montexano, states that this city was constructed in accordance with the design of an earlier model, this due to the apparent speed by which it was built. Support for this comes from US Atlantologist, Kenneth Caroli who writes that this city appears to have been erected by people working from a lost model.

From Greek mythology, that invariably conceals historic fact, comes the story of Dardanus, son of Electra, therefore of Atlantis, his mother being daughter of Atlas. His mother warning him of a coming deluge Dardanus fled to Asia Minor where he settled as king of Troy. The Dardanelles Strait continues to bear his name.

One of the two best regions for amber, worldwide, lie along the English east coast, and coasts of the Baltic Sea, where lies that Finnish Gothland island with it's Cretan maze, magical amber so prized for its lovely decorative effect, but also available from the Atlantic isles of the Azores and Canary whilst not ignoring Madeira. Electra translates as Amber. And who should be revered upon the Atlantic island of Tenerife but Taygete sister to Electra. These sources for amber both Atlantic and Baltic, would have been known to those *Minoan* merchant sea-men by whatever their name's derivation.

Euskotarak.

The above is the name by which Basques refer to themselves.

There is a ceremonial mound in Basque territory near to the city of Biarritz, by the name of Atalya, equivalent of other Atalyas from around the World, even to be found in far-off Mexico. In company with antiquated structures in volcanic stone colours white, red and black, the same name appears where the Guanches are known to have practiced the same witchcraft customs as Basques.

The name Italy is derived from Atalia meaning Domain of Atlas who named his daughter, also known as Electra, Atlantis. It is a name that gives connections for Basques, Guanches, Aztec and Etruscans, alone. It invariably describes a raised mound, even a mountain. It can, too, be seen to indicate that, with the dispersal of the ancient Basques, by land and sea, they reached other lands, particularly South and North America, too, among it's *pre-discovery* Indians. Years ago I read of a scientist who found various similarities between his own tongue and that of the Basques but, despite my recent search, I have failed to pinpoint that source. Never-the-less, I propose that the people, whom we know as the *Minoans*, may well hold the key origin of the Basque Nation, this latter also being Plato's Atlanteans.

I hope that this most- recent result of my research into inexplicable enigmas, from the distant past, will inspire others to investigate areas that I have not recorded, perhaps to find added confirmation for a Basque-*Minoan* nation of Atlanteans. There remains plenty of scope for such confirmation.

A number of unexpected surprises arose throughout my various researched subjects and, to select the most astounding of all is difficult. However, due to the possible far-reaching consequences for historians and the like, I favour the Knossos *trade-marks*, those three examples of a Cretan maze, literally amazing, stark and permanent in their three dimensional forms, giving an historical image to what they represent, and answers for latter-day questions concerning how the people of ancient Knossos obtained tin for manufacture of bronze at least 4,000 years ago.

Bronze-age Crete.

I felt that my investigation might well gain if I could find what became of two groups of related people who vanish from historical records following dispersal, from the Isle of Thera, and what must have been only shortly prior to that volcanic disaster, and later those cousins who left Crete for whatever their reason. Since we have no name by which they were known to one another, my task appeared to be impossible to achieve.

In earlier pages I suggest that people of both Theran and Cretan communities came together to form a cohesive merchant power, operating from a base in the Western Mediterranean Sea-reaches, with proof, at least, for the citizens of Knossos on Crete, that their ships left that Mediterranean Sea to venture into the Atlantic Ocean, those three examples, of a Cretan-maze, supplying proof of that. With a wish to strengthen this theory I turned attention upon the Aegean Bronze Age.

I must thank the efforts of archaeologists for their patient examination of the Palace Period of Crete, that of Knossos among some other quite extensive palaces across that island that attracted careful excavation. Irrespective of that which I hoped to learn, was a factor of which I had no expectations. Evidence had been uncovered of both Cretan and Mycenaean pottery, at a number of distant sites, to westward across the Mediterranean Sea, even as far to west as Eastern Spain, please note. And the French region of Languedoc-Roussillon is so close to that area of Spain, you, may also note. Here, then, is evidence by which to build an extended theory that incorporates Atlantis.

From indeed an early date the people of Crete had organized agriculture in progress, with production of decorated pottery which would become a part of their trading with other lands, in years to come, with Egypt taking a recipients role in that.

At some 2200 BC there commenced an expansion in building the first palaces, Knossos among them. Later signs of Mycenaean influence, in palace architecture, upon Crete, appears to parallel the disappearance of *Minoan* power there, for whatever might be the cause. Although, with the loss of their own homeland, in the region of sixty years previously, it would have been only natural for refugees, from Thera, to seek succour from their closest relations on Crete.

Hearths, for commercial purposes, have been unearthed in Crete. Metal-workers would probably have been itinerates engaged by rich patrons of the merchant class, to create materials for home use and for sale in other lands.

The amount of bronze, discovered in Crete, was very substantial. Yet another intriguing discovery was a generous amount of amber, amber of Baltic origin. Which failed to surprise me.

The amber might have followed an over land route to Crete, but given fair weather in spring, summer and autumn, loads by the ship-ful, would be more convenient. Which, I propose, gave rise to discovery of tin.

Those three examples, of a Cretan maze, direct attention, first to Cornwall where tin was easily extracted from between layers of rock, with the Gulf of Finland further along the sea-route.

Bronze was found at early levels of excavation in Crete. I have now rectified that which the archaeological fraternity will surely not dismiss, out of hand, and hope that my three-maze theory will be found acceptable by them. I reserve my digging to words of print.

A Scandinavian Connection with Atlantis.

A number of publications feature a map of the Isle of Atlantis with a central volcano and six rivers, a depiction upon leather, thought to have originated during the Egyptian Ptolemaic era. But definitely not a Continent. It was discovered by Kircher, a priest with access to the Vatican Library.

Professor of many persuasions, Claus Rudbeck, 1630-1702, and Swedish, spent decades with his investigation of Atlantis, of which he compiled a book upon that especial subject. He wrote that he truly believed that survivors from the Atlantean disaster did reach Sweden, via Finland, now an increasingly plausible theory as recent events may prove. You will recall, that in earlier pages I described what has to be of Cretan origin, a Cretan maze excavated into the surface of Finnish Isle of Gothland, left there by they whom I consider to be ancestors of the Basque population of today.

Much nearer to our time, circa 1960 in fact, Swedish archaeologists discovered signs indicative of an early Bronze-age in their own country, the material with a radio-carbon dating of 2,200 BC. We therefore, have a date contemporaneous with the bronze from the Knossos palace on Crete.

Professor Claus Rudbeck appears to have been a remarkably far-sighted gentleman.

Coincidences.

An all-too-often much-derided word is coincidence. Whereas, for the serious researcher, they provide incidences that must never be carelessly cast aside. Throughout my work quite a number of coincidences have arisen, each occurrence of this given careful consideration, whilst I sought for possible value in them that could provide some further means by which to make progress along this or that exploratory route.

My work commenced with the Sumerian King-lists from which came those numerical divisors with values that coincided with the Stonehenge equivalents. This, in turn, pointed to the Indian Vishnu Epic figure of 432,000 x 4 figure, and the Nordic Valhalla 540 x 800 which also equals 432,000, a numerical route which is littered with repetitions, or a series of coincidences which did not end there. It was by employment of the same mathematical formula that I was able to prove that, the biblical description of Solomon's Temple was, at best, only a record that conceals an insignificant structure, if ever that temple ever existed. Political exaggeration?

In addition to the fore-going comes a strong suspicion that Master Mason Hiram Abiff was not murdered by his apprentices but, rather, provided the sacrificial victim. Might this have involved some type of sacred topping-off process, a final official blessing for completion of the project? With so much editing in the official biblical version the whole deserves serious reconstruction by independent experts. I consider that the planners, at Stonehenge, arrived at their mathematical figures by an independent route.

As to the Cretan maze repetitions, the triple coincidence was, in origin, created to form what one might see as direction-posts for ships to follow when seeking the previously-established sources for tin and amber, therefore making a coincidence only so far as my investigation was concerned.

However, where it relates to similarly-dated discoveries which have no obvious connection, such coincidences deserve close scrutiny.

Forget the myth that events of some type come in threes, since there is not one iota of proof to back that old-wives' tale. Perhaps they should learn to count to four and beyond. But the following can be seen as being strictly three-fold.

You will recall the archaeologically-dated result of excavations at the City of Jaén in Spain. Apart from that is what came to light in similar fashion as a result of a Swedish dig circa 1960.

And there is the date given for the Knossos palace on Crete. How much alike are those related archaeological dates, this apart from the Atlantis ring-structure at the Jaén site?

With allowance made for the increasing accuracy for archaeological dating, all three of the above-named fall around 2200 BC. In addition: was any sign discovered for early manufacture of bronze at Jaén? *Intriguing?*

And I now spoil that three-count with the inclusion of a fourth date, that of the Cornish cliff-side, Cretan maze dated to at least 2000 BC.

Civilization.

Much depends upon the criterion selected for this topic. Experts favour Sumeria as the origin for this, their criterion for that resting upon the ability of that people to make permanent records of all required to sustain their infrastructure, to include agriculture with it's essential irrigation system to be maintained, the various crafts which made life more-comfortable, as well as the creation of tools for all such under-takings, the community's well-being to be guarded against failure of harvest by construction of buildings in which surplus grain could be stored against starvation.

However, a study of the history of Crete reveals reason to question that Sumerian theory. The early arrivals, in Crete, appear to be no -less nor no-more mysterious than those of Egypt and Sumeria, whilst given dates, for this, at least parallel the two afore-mentioned.

Whomsoever was directly involved with the original design, for Stonehenge, had to contend with organization of a large labour force, it's feeding and accommodation, this apart from the establishment of sources with provision for other essential requisites to include tools and some huge blocks of stone. They would also need to set in motion the training of apprentice-initiates in order to ensure continuity, with their Stonehenge project, for the benefit of future generations, information to be broadcast by word of mouth yet retained with the exactitude of the original, a different style in recording, but not available to the non-initiate. If unforced, organization of a work-force can be seen as being civilized.

Upon previous pages I described how construction of Cretan palaces included a means whereby rainwater, falling from roofs, was carefully conducted away to reservoirs of some type, this through a quite modern-looking system of clay-pipes, rather civilized, one might exclaim. Those engineers did have at least one other and clever purpose for such arrangements.

High within a palace walls water-cisterns were installed, keeping in mind that the palaces had first-floor bathrooms. But not only that; they had, too, that which superior citizens of the USA, the finicky type at that, insist upon calling a TOILET, as do many Brits who watch too many TV imports from west of the Atlantic Ocean, or listen to the strange dialogue of weird DJs, of the Wogan-speak image, who, for reasons known only to them, indulge in repetition of all of the latest in idiosyncratic, banal latest in US patois. Time to send some of them into a jungle and forget that they are there, eating disgusting maggots. It used to be that *taking ones toilet* meant a wash or, maybe, a shave, *à la toilette*. Please forgive me the aside.

Within living memory, and doubtless with some that continue to exist within the nether realms of some otherwise civilized countries, including the UK, are small, wooden sheds inside which is a fairly-deep hole, above which, at comfortable seating-level, is wide board, with one or more holes in it, suited to the size of human posteriors, the hole(s) below containing an ample amount of quick-lime which breaks down that which falls upon it.

However, four-thousand years ago palace inhabitants, in Crete, enjoyed all of the comforts provided by flush-lavatories, both at ground-floor level and upstairs, too.

Those cisterns, up above, would permit water, stored within them, to release a controlled amount of water, following the sitter's signal, by whatever the means devised, to flush away human detritus for, maybe, spreading as fertilizer upon the fields. I wonder how any visiting Egyptian dignitary would respond to such a convenience, so enigmatically provided?

So what is your measure for civilization?

I repeat that it is my firm belief that Minoans, as we know them, provide the race of people who are, otherwise, the ancestors of today's Basques.

Incidental.

Is there a subjective element concealed within Plato's description of Atlantis, a numerical factor which may be intended to magnify further the wonders of that isle? I leave it for you to decide.

We are informed that, in size, Atlantis measured 3200 x 2000 Stades. Divide the greater by the lesser, i.e. 3200 ÷ 2000 = 1.6. If my recollection is not at fault this value reflects the perfect proportion of 1.61, otherwise called the Golden Mean, a fitting size for so wondrous an island

However, far from incidental is the following hypothesis -

I return to the story of Theseus and the Minotaur which I translated upon freeing Athens from domination by Crete. I now consider that this should be taken further, in order to correct a misconception of old.

With a Greek Nation, yet to be born, it would be Mycenae, flexing its warlike muscles, that invaded a much-weakened Crete, caused by some type of catastrophe, circa 1470 BC., there for the taking. Merely substitute Mycenaeans for Greeks, Cretan Minoans for Atlanteans, and we have turned full-circle.

With numerical values in mind, if Plato's two measurements for Atlantis are again employed but for purpose of multiplication, we have return to the Sumerian King-lists principal divisor:

3200 x 2000 = 6,400,000 which, in turn, is precisely divisible by 18.604651, and the same once more to a figure of 18490 in readiness for further reduction. Try 43!

My Stonehenge calculations,, in accordance with a friend's estimated figure of some 40.000 - 1, that are in favour of my theory being correct, might be gauged against the positioning of the site's four Station Stones which provide a rectangular design worthy of close examination, particularly when cut into equal parts by the henge's axis. Might this rectangle, with it's provision of some valuable lunar and solar alignments, reveal yet another reason for admiration of some Stone-age mathematician's superb skill?

In the book entitled Stonehenge and Neighbouring Monuments, attention is brought to a Mother Goddess representation carved into the fourth trilithon whilst, upon Trilithon number 2, are carvings of a Mycenaean in style dagger whilst, to it's right, is a bronze axe-head of similarly-suggested provenance. Such implements, in actual bronze, would be from the early Bronze-age which takes us to Crete of 2,200 BC., with British Isles' production commencing circa 1800 BC.

Might it become necessary to modify our present attitudes concerning the pre- history of the Mediterranean BC. era?

An Alternative name for Arthur Evan's Minoan Cretans.

Homer, also when writing of the Pelasgians as inhabitants of Crete, records that perhaps any lack of further detail arises from possible brevity in some aspect of folklore rooted in a time of great antiquity.

My old dictionary refers to Pelasgians as being an ancient race inhabiting coasts and islands of the Eastern Mediterranean Sea with, as is often the case, it being unsafe to assume that one's research, into a specific subject, cannot be further extended, for there may exist, an as yet undetected, mere phrase or word which, when given close examination, will lead to a need to open the mind to a realization that one's investigatory spade has more work awaiting it's already shining blade.

An alternative translation, for Pelagians, is *Folk of the open sea*. Such descriptions are well suited to the early populations of both Crete and Thera

Through the pens of both Homer and Herodotus we reach the Pelasgians who grew in number to inter-marry with other Barbarians.

Homer, in his *Odyssey*, actually places the Pelasgians in Crete. Even so, the Pelasgians appear to have inhabited a wide area of Eastern Aegean lands including Dodona in Epiras, which would become famous for it's Oracle.

When referring further to the Pelasgians, he associates them with the district of Attica with the telling remark that this was dated to a time when *Athenians were first beginning to be accepted as Greeks*, He continues by saying that the Hellenes were not invaders, but were descended from a branch of the Pelasgians who were first few in number until spreading and growing largely by voluntary acceptance of tribes of *Barbarians* into their company. To Hellenic Greeks *Barbarian* meant solely people of less-refined nature or culture.

From both early and modern day sources the Pelasgians are seen as pre-Hellenic occupiers of land and isles in the Eastern Mediterranean vicinity, a people who must now become serious contenders for those whose magnificent constructions, in Crete, commence circa early 3rd. Millennium BC, a race which appears to be uninfluenced by other cultures of that era, an inventive race, highly-intelligent, their creations standing alone, their palace- constructions bearing a uniqueness that might be seen to be quite modern in some among the techniques employed. It is also proposed that the Pelasgians left Asia Minor en route to the Aegean basin as early as the 5th Millennium BC.

Strange to say, these people have no aspects, in mythology, that have correspondences within the Europe or Asia Minor of their era. Whatsoever their yet-to-be established origin I believe that the name Pelasgian to be the same by which Arthur Evan's *Minoans* were known among themselves and neighbouring tribes.

It becomes increasingly-evident that, much considered to be Greek in origin, has roots firmly-set in the much earlier Cretan culture, with a far-too loose usage of the former in terms of historic inaccuracy. The term Minoan is an example of this. Television has much with which to answer in this regard

The Lunar Goddess in Triad and Matriarchal Domination.

When Robert Graves' The White Goddess was first published there were those who were far too eager to condemn it out-of-hand, doubtless the types who feared that belief in a male superiority, from earliest of days, was about to be completely destroyed, they of the Christian Brotherhood types whose Adam must be seen as being far-more noble than Eve, a mere opportunist seductress. But that Creation was simply a device employed to provide *proof* that The Goddess never was.

In support of Grave's White Goddess there are other works, drawn from Indo-European sources, from mythology and as result of archaeological enterprise.

Artemis, formerly from Crete, had, among her many charming epithets, *She of the Three Ways*, here to be seen as the Triple Goddess in her three guises of Virgin, Nubile Woman and Wise Crone.

There is, too, *Selene of the Three Faces. The Three Charities, The Three Moirae, The Three Erinyes, The Three Graces, The Three Furies, The Three Fates. Hecate, too, is Goddess of the Morn, Mother of All, and Goddess of the Night.*

Goddess worship is strongly reflected in the Monk's poem, from a previous page.

There is much from ancient tradition to symbolize worship of lunar trinities from long prior to the invention of all-powerful male divinities. Whilst Rome has it's own Trinity.

Israelis tell of a *God-given* right to occupy the whole of former Palestine, a male deity, naturally. Yet they fail to widely publicise their evidence, from archaeological sources, the various remains of temples to goddess-figures discovered in the Holy Land which are most-likely to pre-date ancestors of King David and company.

Not to be outdone, Shakespeare tells of *Three Weird Sisters*.

The Norse Norns are goddesses who control not solely the fates of men but also *keep gods in their lowly places*. They are goddesses of *Destiny* who guard the *Never-changing laws of the Cosmos,* and are three in number by the names of *Urd, Verdandi* and *Skuld*.

Elsewhere is a trio of winged maidens, avengers who pursue perpetrators of crime, three lovely ladies known as *Alecto the Uneasy, Tisphone the Blood Avenger and Megaera the Denyer*, equivalents of the Greek *Erinyes*.

Athene, Hera and Aphrodite, needless to say, form yet another triad. So beware of that three-threes you players of cards, 9 is the number of sisters, with Morgan Le Fay at their head, who placed the corpse of King Arthur upon a barge to be carried to the Sepulchral Isle of Apples. Morgan is a fairy, a queen and, elsewhere, a goddess.

No matter the lack of named triadic-goddesses, a lunar influence was behind composition of those Sumerian King-lists. Similarly the Indian Vishnu Epic, that reached to Cambodia to the east, is also lunar related, as is the construction of Solomon's Temple. And, as for Stonehenge, the mathematics are proof enough.

Reference Sources.

Old Coventry and Lady Godiva.
Author; F. Burbridge.

The White Goddess. Publishers: Faber and Faber. 1961 edition.
Author; Robert Graves.

The Greek Myths; Volumes 1 and 2. Penguin Books. 1960 edition.
Author:: Robert Graves.

The Golden Bough; 1993. Wordsworth Editions Limited.
Author; J.G. Frazer.

The Holy Blood and the Holy Grail. Corgi Books.1984 Edition.
Authors; Michael Baigent, Richard Leigh and Henry Lincoln.

Arthurian Legend. Element Books Limited.1991 Edition.
Author; Ronan Coghian.

Monk's Poem. The British Museum.
MS. Harley. 1585 if 12v 13r.

Rennes Ie Château. A Visitor's Guide. 1993 Edition.
Publishers; Tatiana   Kletzy-Pradere.

New Larousse Encyclopaedia of Mythology. English Edition, 1983.
Publishers; The Hamlyn Publishing Group Limited.

The End of Atlantis. Publishers: Thames and Hudson.
Author; V. Luoe.

The Birth of Europe. 1991.
Author; Michael Andrews.

BBC Book. The Megalithic Odyssey.
Publishers; Türnstone Press Limited.
Autho;: Christain O'Brien.

Stonehenge Complete. Paper-back.1985 edition.
Publishers; Thames and Hudson.

The Golden Age of Myth and Legend.
Wordsworth Editions Ltd. 1943.
Author; Thomas Bullfinch.

Ancient Britain. Myths and Legend. 1995 edition.
Publisher Chancellor Press.
Author; M.I. Ebutt.

—